Words of Fire; Rivers of Tears

Words of Fire; Rivers of Tears

THE MAN JEREMIAH

David M. Howard

TYNDALE
House Publishers, Inc.
Wheaton, Illinois
COVERDALE
House Publishers, Ltd.
London, England

Library of Congress Catalog Card Number 75-37233
ISBN 8423-8480-4, paper

First printing, January 1976.
Printed in the United States of America.

To my mother, who has paid the price and who knows the joy of praying all six of her children into the service of the God of Jeremiah

Contents

PART FOUR: Christ and Jeremiah

Foreword

I have not kept track of how many preachers I have heard since I became a Christian twenty-five years ago. I have, however, kept track of those few whose ministry God used in my own life, not just to bring another message, but to inspire encouragement, vision, and new hope. David Howard is one of these.

Across sixteen years of missionary service I saw many field conferences come and go. Ho hum! But the 1967 conference was different from the others. David Howard, then a missionary in Colombia with the Latin America Mission, came to Cochabamba, Bolivia, as our conference speaker. His messages, drawing out personal and practical implications of the lives of men and women in the Bible, were electrifying. They warmed my heart, while (I must admit) they often rattled my cage. But God used them in a special way. I have not been the same since.

You can expect a similar experience as you read this book. I have seen dozens of books on the prophet Jeremiah that help me learn more about Jeremiah, and I appreciate them very much. But here is one that makes Jeremiah a mirror into which I, the reader, look and as a result come to understand myself better. How desperately I need that. How grateful I am to God that David Howard's Spirit-filled pulpit ministry is now being multiplied through the printed page to thousands who will never have the privilege of hearing him personally!

9

FOREWORD

Jeremiah was a godly man. So is David Howard. Put them both together and the combination carries a tremendous spiritual wallop. I like the way David dares to write in the first person, leaving himself vulnerable—just like Jeremiah. That makes it easier for you and me to identify with both of them and thus to open our own hearts for a fresh ministry of the Spirit.

The versatility of these soul-stirring applications of the Old Testament Scriptures amazes me. I wish I had seen Jeremiah in this light when I was a new Christian. I would have been more useful to God and to other people if I had. I think this book should be read as a Sunday school textbook far and wide. A Sunday school teacher who uses this book for a three-month study, developing discussion questions appropriate to the group, can expect the class, whether high schoolers or senior citizens, to make great strides in their spiritual lives and in their ability to serve their Lord.

C. Peter Wagner
Fuller Theological Seminary
School of World Mission

Preface

This is a book about a man, a man named Jeremiah.

It is not a book about a book. That is, it is not a commentary on the Book of Jeremiah. Rather it is reflections on the life of a man who lived during a vital period of history, at a crucial place, and who experienced the ordinary as well as the overwhelming problems that face the servants of the Lord.

God's call to Jeremiah, his response to that call, and the consequences of that response all come to life when one looks at Jeremiah as a very ordinary man. His hopes and aspirations, the messages he gave both of dire warning and of great triumph, the bitter opposition and hatred which surrounded him, the defeats and failures which he suffered—all ring true. Every honest servant of the Lord will sooner or later go through some (although hopefully not all!) of the things which Jeremiah encountered.

While it may not be the lot of the average Christian in the Western world to end up in the stocks or the slime pits, it is well to remember that our brethren in other parts of the world today are experiencing precisely this type of treatment—and even far worse. And it may help us to handle better those disappointments and crushing tragedies which so often do enter our lives if we can see how Jeremiah responded to the hand of God upon him.

Here is a man who lived almost constantly with suffering and failure, yet who never lost his faith in the One who called him before he was formed in his mother's womb. Here is a man who paid the price of proclaiming faithfully an unpopular message from God. And here is a man who wept, both publicly and privately, because of his deep love for and identification with his people.

He was, as one writer called him, "the supreme prophet of the human heart."

We need more such prophets today!

David M. Howard

Acknowledgments

I am deeply thankful for my wife, Phyllis, who is a constant source of encouragement in stimulating me to further study of the Scriptures to be shared with others.

I wish to express my gratitude to my colleagues on the staff of Inter-Varsity Christian Fellowship, especially those in the southeastern United States who were the first recipients of these studies. Their response to Jeremiah as a man and to the Word of God as expressed by Jeremiah encouraged me to prepare these reflections for wider use. I am also grateful to Kay Barton, who typed and edited the manuscript and checked all Scripture references. The editors at Tyndale House have also been very helpful in putting this book into readable form.

If Jeremiah can become a living man to other servants of the Lord and can encourage them as he has done for me, I shall be amply rewarded.

PART ONE

The Call of Jeremiah

The words of Jeremiah, the son of Hilkiah, of the priests who were in Anathoth in the land of Benjamin, to whom the word of the Lord came in the days of Josiah the son of Amon, king of Judah, in the thirteenth year of his reign. It came also in the days of Jehoiakim the son of Josiah, king of Judah, and until the end of the eleventh year of Zedekiah, the son of Josiah, king of Judah, until the captivity of Jerusalem in the fifth month.

Now the word of the Lord came to me saying, "Before I formed you in the womb I knew you, and before you were born I consecrated you; I appointed you a prophet to the nations." Then I said, "Ah, Lord God! Behold, I do not know how to speak, for I am only a youth." But the Lord said to me, "Do not say, 'I am only a youth'; for to all to whom I send you you shall go, and whatever I command you you shall speak. Be not afraid of them, for I am with you to deliver you, says the Lord." Then the Lord put forth his hand and touched my mouth; and the Lord said to me, "Behold, I have put my words in your mouth. See, I have set you this day over nations and over kingdoms, to pluck up and to break down, to destroy and to overthrow, to build and to plant." And the word of the Lord came to me, saying, "Jeremiah, what do you see?" And I said, "I see a rod of almond." Then the Lord said to me, "You have seen well, for I am watching over my word to perform it."

Jeremiah 1:1-12

CHAPTER ONE

"Before I Formed You, I Knew You"

The Foundation of God's Call

God seems to delight in using the most unlikely prospects in His work. This is seen in the physical and the intellectual realm. Those that were voted in the high school yearbook "most likely to succeed" don't necessarily do so, and some of those we think least likely to succeed are the ones who often do.

One night my wife and I were invited to a banquet honoring the Wheaton College wrestling coach, who was retiring after nearly thirty years of coaching. A number of his former wrestlers were there. We had a lot of fun reminiscing over the good times we had had together.

While I was in graduate school, I had been his assistant coach. We were reminiscing that night about one man who was certainly the least likely wrestler I have ever seen. He was six feet, one inch tall and was wrestling the 121-pound class! When he came out for wrestling, I was sure that he would never make it. But the poor fellow tried

17

so hard. He wanted desperately to make the team. I can remember going home in the evenings and saying to my wife, "Poor John doesn't stand a chance of ever making it as a wrestler."

But John was determined, and by the end of his senior year he was awarded the Dawson Trophy, given each year to the outstanding wrestler. He had determined that he *was* going to make it. He was one of those least likely to succeed who finally *did* succeed.

Look into the Scriptures and you see the kind of person that God chose. Frequently, considering their background, you would not have selected them as likely to excel.

Joseph, the eleventh of twelve brothers, was sold into slavery in Egypt by his brothers. What could he amount to?

What was Moses doing when God spoke to him? He was keeping the flocks of another man, which he had been doing for forty years. He didn't even have his own flock of sheep. There he was—just a hired servant to his father-in-law—out in the desert.

Samuel was just a young boy who helped clean up in the Temple, opened the doors in the morning, closed them at night, lit the lamps, put out the lamps. He was a rather insignificant servant in the Temple.

David was the youngest of seven brothers and certainly the least likely to succeed. His father as much as said so. "I've got one more left. I don't know why you would want to see him. He is out there taking care of the sheep."

What was Elisha doing? Plowing with oxen when Elijah came along and threw his mantle over him. He was a plowman, a rather unlikely candidate to become a fiery prophet.

18

And who was Esther? A humble Jewish maiden living in captivity in another land under a foreign government.

Peter, Andrew, James, John—what were they doing when Jesus came along? Mending their fishing nets.

And Paul? What was he doing? Executing the Christians! Scarcely a proper preparation for becoming an apostle!

Go right down the line and pick out the people whom God chose to serve Him and frequently, on the basis of their background, they would not have been the ones that you or I would have chosen. But when God calls a person, He has His own plans and His own ways of doing things.

If you study how God called different people in Scripture, you will find all kinds of different angles to God's call. Every call differs. But there are certain things which I believe will always be present.

First, there is what God has done in the past to prepare the person for His call. Second, there will be that person's response. How does he react to what God says to him? And third, there will be God's response to that. How does God move on the basis of that person's response?

God prepares the way to lay His hand upon a person. When that man or woman responds to God, then God responds to them. Those three elements will always be found in the call of a man or woman of God in Scripture, and in our lives.

The foundation of God's call to Jeremiah is found in the opening verses of his book.

> Now the word of the Lord came to me saying, "Before I formed you in the womb I knew you, and before you were born I consecrated you; I appointed you a prophet to the nations." (Jeremiah 1:4, 5)

19

God did three things before He ever got around to calling Jeremiah. He mentions them right here. "Before I formed you in the womb I *knew* you." God is in effect saying, "Before you were born—even before you were conceived—I *knew* you. I knew all about you. I knew who you were, I knew what you would become, and I knew what I wanted to do through you." In our minds we know that to be true. Yes, God knows everything. He is omniscient. He knows the beginning. He knows the end from the beginning. We accept all of that intellectually. But just stop and think for a moment. What does that mean to you personally? Before you were ever conceived in your mother's womb, God *knew* you.

English is sometimes a limited language in its power of expression. Some other languages occasionally have a richer way of expressing truth. There are a number of different biblical words that can be translated by our English word "to know." The one used here is the same word found in Deuteronomy 34:10 at the end of Moses' life when we read:

> And there has not arisen a prophet since in Israel like Moses, whom the Lord knew face to face.

There has never been a man before or since, the Word of God says, whom God *knew* as He knew Moses face to face. That is the word used here about Jeremiah. It is a word which implies the most intimate relationship which could exist. No man in the Old Testament ever knew God in the personal way that Moses did. But God says, "I *knew* Jeremiah in that way before he was born."

This same word is found in Nahum 1:7:

> The Lord is good, a stronghold in the day of trouble; he knows those who take refuge in him.

Those who come to Him are the ones that He *knows* in a
very intimate and personal way.

So God says to Jeremiah, "Before you were born I knew
you, just as I knew Moses face to face." "Before you were
born I knew you, as the one who takes refuge in Me."

This is the same concept expressed in different words
in Romans 8:29:

> For those whom he foreknew he also predestined to
> be conformed to the image of his Son....

Those that He knew beforehand, He predestined in
His eternal counsels to become like Christ.

Thus when God says "I knew you," it means intimate,
personal acquaintance. It speaks of loving care—"the ones
who take refuge in Me, I know as a loving Father." It is
the sovereign determination of God—"I foreknew all
about you and, therefore, I determined that you should be
conformed to the image of My Son." That is the word that
is used here.

The New English Bible translates it this way: "Before
you were born I knew you for my own." God is saying, "I
knew you personally. I wanted you to be Mine."

Have you ever become excited because you were
recognized by someone that you didn't expect would
know you? When I was a new missionary in Costa Rica, I was
assigned, in my third term of language school, to write a
paper on the politics of Costa Rica. So I went to the
University and interviewed some professors to discover
what the politics of Costa Rica were all about. They said,
"There is really only one significant politician in this
country. If you want to understand politics, go to see
him."

I said, "Who is it?"

21

"President Figueres."

He had just been elected President but had not yet taken office. He happened to live at that time, before moving into the presidential palace, right across the street from our language school. So one day, as a brash young student, I walked across the street and rang his doorbell.

His secretary came to the door and I said, "I would like to see President Figueres."

He said, "Fine, come right in."

He ushered me into the living room, and five minutes later in walked President Figueres.

He said, "How are you, young man? Glad to see you. What can I do for you?"

He sat down, and we had a long chat. I told him that I wanted to learn about the politics of Costa Rica. He gave me quite an introduction to politics in general and his views in particular. It was a fascinating time. On several occasions after that, I met President Figueres and to my amazement, he always knew me.

A year or so later, our second child was born in our mission hospital. President Figueres' wife also gave birth to a child the next day in the same hospital. She was billeted in the room next to my wife. The President and I met in the hallway as we paced the floor together. He knew me and called me by name. Later on, we met at a reception and again at an outdoor ceremony. And he always seemed to remember me. I was astounded.

Have you ever stopped to realize who God is when He says, "I knew you"? It is one thing to have the president of a country recognize you. But this is the Creator of the universe who says, "I knew you. I know you now. I know you by name. I know how many hairs there are in your head. I know all about you." And that is God's Word to us today.

22

"I know you in a very intimate and personal way."

He goes on to say, "Before you were born I consecrated you." The word "consecrated" means to be set aside, sanctified for a specific purpose. "Before you were born I set you aside."

Did it ever occur to you that before you were born, God decided that you were to be involved in the work which you are presently doing? He looked down across the years and saw that you were the person that He wanted to assign to a specific job. And before you were born, He set you aside to do that job. He knew all about you and He consecrated you.

> For we are his workmanship, created in Christ Jesus unto good works, which God hath before ordained that we should walk in them. (Eph. 2:10, KJV)

Before the foundation of the world, He ordained those works in which we should walk.

CHAPTER TWO

"I Am Only a Youth"

The Response to God's Call

God goes on to say to Jeremiah, "I appointed you a prophet to the nations. I had this job in mind for you long before you were born."

How much did Jeremiah have to do with this call? How much choice did he have? This happened even before he was conceived! There was no way that Jeremiah could enter into this original plan. He had no choice in the matter. God appointed him to be a prophet long before he was born.

At Urbana 73 Elisabeth Elliot Leitch, speaking about the place of women in missions, made this statement: "We have nothing to do with the *choice* of the gift. We have everything to do with the *use* of the gift."

You had nothing to do with choosing whether you are a man or a woman. Likewise, you had nothing to do with choosing a lot of other things about your life, such as the spiritual gifts that have been given to you. But you have everything to do with the *use* of those gifts. Jeremiah had no choice in being named a prophet. Jeremiah had everything to do with how he responded to being named a prophet. And that is where you and I fit in. We are fully responsible for our response to what God has already appointed us to do.

How, then, did Jeremiah respond? We have seen the foundation of God's call. This is something God did long before Jeremiah was born, way back in the eternal counsels of the Godhead. But how does Jeremiah respond? It is our response to that call which determines much of our personal development.

> Then I said, "Ah, Lord God! Behold, I do not know how to speak, for I am only a youth." (Jeremiah 1:6)

That is a very human type of response. And, in a sense, it is rather predictable. It is natural and comes so easily. "Lord, I can't do this. I'm too young, too inexperienced."

At different times in your own development you have, no doubt, been overwhelmed with a feeling of inadequacy. Right after graduation from college I joined the staff of Inter-Varsity Christian Fellowship. I had a Christian college background and now I was turned loose on the secular campuses. This can be a pretty rough way to go at times. I also had the misfortune, in those days, of looking about the age of a high school senior. I would go onto a campus and students would think, at best, that I was some new freshman or perhaps some high school student who was coming to see the campus. That was an embarrassing burden for me to bear. I was called Missions Staff Member. I had the whole country to cover and thus traveled all over the U. S. and Canada.

I can remember, for example, getting off the train in eastern Washington to visit a university. Just two of us got off the train at that stop. The other man was middle-aged. The student who had come to meet me had heard that the Missions Staff Member of Inter-Varsity was coming, so he was looking for some gray-haired missionary, I guess. He stepped immediately up to the older man and said, "Mr. Howard?"

The gentleman looked perplexed and said, "No."

I stepped up and said, "I think I am the one you are looking for."

"You?" He sort of backed off. "You're Dave Howard?"

I said, "Yes. Sorry to disappoint you, but I am Dave Howard."

The poor fellow was completely flustered, and that didn't help build my ego either. I suffered through that sort of thing constantly. Again and again I would find myself saying, "Lord, I can't do this. I am only a youth. I'm supposed to be a Missions Staff Member talking about missions. I have never been a missionary. I have never even visited the mission field. I don't know how to do this job."

Perhaps you have been going through the same problem. You say, "I am too young for this, Lord. Why did you place me in this kind of a job? This is one time you really made a mistake."

The same experience was repeated for me often on the mission field. After our first term in Costa Rica, the Latin America Mission asked us to transfer to Colombia. I was open to that, but I wasn't particularly anxious to do so. I had enjoyed my work in Costa Rica. I had a responsible position, good opportunities, and was satisfied. Then they asked me to move to Colombia and become Field Director.

27

This meant directing people who were twenty years my senior, both in age and in experience on the field. During our first year in Colombia, over and over again in the dark thoughts of my own heart, I would struggle with this. I found myself saying, "Lord, this was one time you really erred. Why did you send me to Colombia to a job like this?" I remember thinking Kenneth Strachan (our mission's General Director) didn't know what he was doing this time. He had given me a job I was incapable of doing. I felt too young and out of place. I felt very much like Jeremiah, "Ah, Lord God! Behold, I do not know how to speak, for I am only a youth."

I look back now with deep thankfulness for the wonderful years that God gave us in Colombia. God made no mistake. I was the one who was mistaken. But at that time, I felt completely incapable of doing the job. Do you feel that way in your present responsibilities? Well, you are in good company, for that is the way Jeremiah felt.

How did God respond to Jeremiah's feelings of inadequacy? If you are identifying with Jeremiah in saying, "Lord, I don't know how to speak. I am only a youth," listen to the Lord who says:

> ..."Do not say, 'I am only a youth'; for to all to whom I send you you shall go, and whatever I command you you shall speak. Be not afraid of them, for I am with you to deliver you, says the Lord."
> (Jeremiah 1:7, 8)

These are great words of encouragement! Notice the relationship between what God does and how we should respond.

God's part is: I am going to send you. Our part is: Go.

God's part is: I am going to command you. Our part is: Speak.

God's part is: I am going to be with you. Our part is: Be not afraid.

Who sent you out into that job you now hold? It wasn't the president of your organization. It wasn't your immediate supervisor. Basically, you are there by the appointment of God, because God sent you. Therefore, you go. You go with boldness. You go with confidence. You go because God said, "For to all to whom I send you you shall go."

And what do you say when you get to those to whom God has sent you? What do you say when you are trying to encourage other Christians in their personal growth? What do you say when you are talking to non-Christians who are bringing up arguments you never heard of before and you don't know how to answer?

"Whatever I command you you shall speak." So you say to them what God has said to you through His Word. You no doubt have a lot more to learn. All of us do. But you speak the words that God has spoken to you through His Word. "I am the one who commands you," says God, "and, therefore, you speak by my authority and not by the authority of anyone else."

"But," you say, "I am so frightened when I try to speak for God."

And God answers, "Don't be afraid of them. I am with you to deliver you."

Have you ever been so frightened that you hardly knew what to say? Probably you have. I have too.

One night at the University of Wisconsin, I was asked to speak on witchcraft and demonism. After the meeting, a fellow came up and began to question me. It soon became obvious that he was deeply involved in witchcraft and, as he put it, had sold himself—body, soul, and spirit—to the Devil. He had offered a sacrifice of his own blood, which had been drunk by his fellow witches. He described in the most gruesome details what he had gone through.

He finally asked, with deep feeling, "Can a man who has sold his soul to the Devil ever be delivered?" I realized that we were in the presence of demon powers. In hindsight I believe that he was demon-possessed. What do you do when you are looking into the eyes of a demon-possessed person?

By the way (and I cannot urge this too strongly), never try to handle this alone if it can possibly be avoided. It is no light matter to be in the presence of evil powers. It is not to be trifled with. Whenever possible, we need the presence and help of another Christian. Don't try to stand alone in the face of satanic power. Seek the strength and help of a fellow-member of the body of Christ.

An Inter-Varsity student prayed for an hour and a half while I tried to help the young man understand how to be delivered from the power of Satan. It was a traumatic experience. He went through agonizing physical upheavals similar to what the Gospel of Mark describes about demon-possessed people. But the Lord wonderfully delivered him and today he is a radiant Christian.

At a later date I asked him if he had had any further involvement in witchcraft. He said, "Absolutely not," then added, "I stay totally away from that except to warn people to stay out of it."

Looking back on that night, I realize I was so frightened I hardly knew what to do. And yet the Lord's Word was, "Be not afraid of them, for I am with you to deliver you." When you find yourself in a situation which frightens you, remember the words of the Lord, "Don't be afraid. I am with you to deliver you."

If you want an exciting study, take a concordance, go through the Scriptures, and see how often God says "Fear not." Study the times, the places, and the circumstances in which He said that.

Take, for example, the beautiful Christmas story. There had been 400 silent years after the closing of the Old Testament. The prophetic words had ceased. No prophets were raised up, and for 400 years God did not speak through new revelation. Israel lived in silence. They wondered if perhaps God had forgotten them. The people of Israel were echoing the words of the Psalmist:

> Has his steadfast love for ever ceased? Are his promises at an end for all time? Has God forgotten to be gracious? Has he in anger shut up his compassion? (Psalm 77:8, 9)

They probably began to wonder, "Didn't God really mean all the things He said in the Old Testament?"

Then one day a priest named Zechariah (or Zacharias) went into the Temple in his normal tour of duty. Suddenly an angel appeared beside him. For the first time in 400 years God broke through, and out of the silence of those years He spoke to His people Israel. Notice the first words that He said: "Fear not."

> But the angel said unto him, Fear not, Zacharias: for thy prayer is heard; and thy wife Elisabeth shall bear thee a son, and thou shalt call his name John. (Luke 1:13, KJV)

God knows exactly when to speak those words. He always speaks them at the right time. Zechariah was among those

31

who, perhaps, were becoming fearful and were wondering, "Well, did God really mean it?" And God says, "Zechariah, fear not. I meant what I said and I am going to carry it out."

Three more times in the Christmas story, we find those words "Fear not."

To the Virgin Mary, greatly troubled by the appearance of Gabriel who announced the incomprehensible news of her special place among women as the mother of the Messiah, the angel said:

> ...Fear not, Mary: for thou hast found favor with God. (Luke 1:30, KJV)

To Joseph, who was perplexed and deeply disturbed by his fiancée's unexpected condition, the angel of the Lord in kindness said,

> ...Joseph, thou son of David, fear not to take unto thee Mary thy wife: for that which is conceived in her is of the Holy Ghost. (Matthew 1:20, KJV)

Then to the humble shepherds in the field, who were filled with fear at the glory of the Lord, the angel graciously said,

> Fear not: for, behold, I bring you good tidings of great joy, which shall be to all people. (Luke 2:10, KJV)

And so God says to you and to me today, when He calls us to do His work, "Don't be afraid, for I am with you to deliver you."

CHAPTER THREE

"I Am Watching over My Word"

The Assurance That Accompanies God's Call

When God calls a person, He has prepared the way. But
that person must respond. Then God gives assurance of
what He is going to do.

> Then the Lord put forth his hand and touched my
> mouth; and the Lord said to me, "Behold, I have put
> my words in your mouth." (Jeremiah 1:9)

What a promise! "Jeremiah, when you go out to speak
as a prophet, as I have appointed you to do, you are going
to speak words which I will put in your mouth."

The job description for an Inter-Varsity staff member
says that he is a man (or woman) who comes with a word
from God. If he has no word from God, he has no business
going onto the campus. If he doesn't know what it is to hear
God speak and to speak for God, he is out of place on
Inter-Varsity staff. He is not appointed to Inter-Varsity

staff until there is evidence that he knows what it is to receive things from God and to share them with others.

God says to Jeremiah, "I have put my words in your mouth."

Have you ever had one of those experiences where you had no idea what you were going to say and yet somehow the words came? It can be exciting, but it isn't the kind of thing that we should count on all the time. In other words, if I have a speaking engagement, I must not assume that no preparation is necessary because God will give me the words. That's not it at all. But there will be occasions when something arises for which you are totally unprepared. When that happens, you can be sure that God will give you the necessary words. Then there will be that exciting sense that this is a word from God.

Some years ago in Colombia, we got caught in the midst of a very confusing situation. There was a wonderful movement of the Holy Spirit developing. Then suddenly along with it came some of the worst conceivable extremes and perversions, such as satanic imitations of the gifts of the Holy Spirit. There was also demonic activity that misled the church. It became the most confused situation that I had ever seen. We did not know how to straighten it out. We knew that the Spirit of God was at work. We knew equally well that the Devil was at work. We needed to sort out what was from God and what was from the Devil.

Churches began to divide over this. There were those who believed that certain gifts belonged to every Christian, and unless you had those gifts you hadn't reached Christian maturity, or maybe you weren't even a Christian. There were others who felt none of this is for the Christian—it's all of the Devil. Throw all of them in the same pot and an explosion is inevitable!

34

Finally they decided to discuss this issue at the annual church convention. I arrived on a Monday and noticed on the agenda for the next day a major address entitled "The Position of the Latin America Mission Facing the Charismatic Movement." My name was listed to give that address. I had not been requested to do this, nor had I any idea that this was coming. We did not have an official position in the Latin America Mission. We hadn't struggled through this question yet. We didn't know which way to turn. I was 100 miles from my home where my books and files were located. I had no recourse to those study tools, and here I was within twenty-four hours of a major address on our position.

My first reaction was to say, "No, I can't do it. You didn't ask me to do this. You gave me no preparation. I won't do it."

Then it seemed as though the Lord said, "Now look. Here's a great opportunity. Here are 200 representatives of the churches from all over northern Colombia. Here is a great chance to try to bring them together on this controversial point."

During the first day the tensions were building up. I remember our first time of prayer. Many of the people enjoyed praying out loud together. But others rejected the practice as not being true prayer. Just before we went to prayer, one man stood up and said, "Now wait a minute. Before we go to prayer, I want to know if this is going to be a real prayer meeting or a shouting match."

Another man stood up and said, "Unless we all pray out loud together, it isn't real prayer."

Someone else stood up and said, "The only way to pray is with one person leading so everyone else can listen and go along with him."

THE CALL OF JEREMIAH

This went back and forth with tension building up more and more.

Finally one man stood up and pointing across the room at me said, "I want the Director of the Latin America Mission to tell us what true prayer is." I made a few brief comments about "where the Spirit of the Lord is, there is liberty."

I had no idea what to say in my address the next day. I hardly slept that night. I tried to sketch down a few thoughts on a piece of paper, but I had no real substance developed. I called my wife in the city where we lived and asked her to get the missionaries there to pray for me.

At one o'clock the next afternoon, I called together the missionaries who were at the convention and asked them to pray for me. I explained what I would basically try to say, although I really had no idea how this would develop. While we were praying, the Lord gave me a very wonderful word of encouragement.

In that prayer meeting, God graciously gave the gift of prophecy to a student from Princeton who was visiting us on a short-term basis. It was a word from God assuring me that He was going to give me the words needed. This student very quietly prayed in tongues, clearly, with no gibberish. When he finished praying, he was immediately given the interpretation. It was such a beautiful word directly for me that I asked him later if he would write it down. This is what was said:

> Am I not sovereign, saith the Lord?
> Are not these my people? (The emphasis was, "Dave, they are not *your* people. You don't have to carry this burden. They are my people.")
> Do I not look down on them with eyes of love?

I have put upon you my yoke for them. (In other
words, "You have to do this, Dave. I have placed
my yoke upon you.")
And is not my yoke easy, saith the Lord?
For I am in the yoke with you, shouldering the
burden. (They use yokes in Colombia for oxen.
Yokes are always double. You never see one ox
pulling a cart. It is always two oxen. And the word
was, "Dave, I put my yoke upon you, but a yoke has
two sides. I am in the other side, pulling my part of
the load with you.")

Rest in me;
Look unto me;
I will shepherd my people,
For I am willing and able to watch over my flock.

I felt like Christian in *Pilgrim's Progress* when he reached
the Cross and the burden rolled off his shoulders. I almost
felt physically the rolling away of a heavy burden that had
been crushing me.

I rose from that prayer meeting and I went across the
conference grounds to the tabernacle where two hundred
people were gathered. I got up to speak, still not
knowing for sure what I was going to say. Yet I spoke for
an hour with a greater sense of freedom and liberty than I can
remember at any prior time in my ministry.

Afterwards some of my colleagues testified, "Dave,
God never gave you greater liberty or greater power than
He gave you today." This was no credit to me. It was simply
one of those cases where God says, "I have put my words
in your mouth. Now you speak those words."

God will do this when you are caught in those situations

where you have to have that word from God. "I will put my words in your mouth."

Secondly, God says:

> "See, I have set you this day over nations and over kingdoms...." (Jeremiah 1:10a)

That's authority! God gives a message and the authority to speak the message.

We don't know much about Jeremiah as a man. He was probably quite young at this time. He may have been around twenty. At least we know that he ministered for more than forty years after that. Here is this young man who says, "I am only a youth. I can't speak." But God says, "I am placing you over nations and over kingdoms. I am putting you over the rulers of this nation. I am placing you in a position higher than the king himself." What a staggering thought! "I am placing you *over* those who are in authority. I am giving you a higher authority, which comes from Me." When you speak the words that God puts in your mouth, you speak with the authority that comes from God. And that authority cannot be stopped.

I used to thrill in seeing people who were commanded not to speak in the name of the Lord, yet daring to do so on the basis of a higher authority. I remember a lady coming to me in Colombia during the years of violent persecution there. She showed me a letter signed by an ecclesiastical authority of that area. She was holding meetings in her home as there was no evangelical church in her little village. A group of Christians would come to her home and worship the Lord together. The letter said:

> I wish to say to you that out of love, I am warning you not to open your home again for

Protestant services; because I have received some
complaints about your meetings and they assured
me that they will not be responsible for what
might happen, and that they only hoped that I
would advise you, so that they can proceed with the
purpose which they have against the preachers of
Macaján, be it you or men from Sincelejo; and
the most beautiful part is that if anything happens
to your lives, I will not permit the law to punish
anyone; first they would have to punish me, and
those interested will continue fighting;
therefore the most prudent course would be to
stop [these services] for the safety of your lives, since
the life of man is such a precious gift from God. I
did not discover this plot, but according to what
they have given me to understand, it includes
death and burning of the house where services are
held; thus it is better to prevent than to cure, and it
is my duty to warn you; I am keeping a copy of
this for what may transpire in defense of those
involved.

[signed] Father Luis Jaramillo

I didn't know what to say to her, so I asked, "What do
you plan to do?"

And with a great smile on her face, she said, "I am going to
go right on with those meetings, because my authority
comes from God."

And she did. In this case she was delivered. There were
many other Colombians during that period who refused to
remain silent. They spoke because there was a higher
authority which they refused to disobey. Some died as a
result. You may never be called upon to die for your faith,

but I hope you will never give in to a lesser authority than the authority of God who told you to speak the words that "I put in your mouth."

And then finally:

> And the word of the Lord came to me, saying, "Jeremiah, what do you see?" And I said, "I see a rod of almond." Then the Lord said to me, "You have seen well, for I am watching over my word to perform it." (Jeremiah 1:11, 12)

What is the relationship between a rod of almond and God watching over His Word? This is one of those cases where English cannot express exactly what is said. There is a play on words here. Most Hebrew words are based on a root of three letters. There are two words used here. The word for "rod of almond" is *shaqued.* The word "to watch" is *shoqued.* It is the same three root letters with different vowel pointings. It is a form of pun with the Lord saying, *"Shaqued"*—a rod of almond; *"shoqued"*—"I am watching over my word to perform it."

What God is saying is, "Jeremiah, see this rod of almond? I want it to say to you that I, the Creator of the universe, am watching over my word to perform it. Remember, I put my words in your mouth. Now I am watching over those words. In the final analysis, the responsibility is mine, not yours."

You and I are sent out under the authority of God with a message from God. But the final responsibility is God's, not ours.

> I planted, Apollos watered, but God gave the growth. (1 Cor. 3:6)

We can't give the increase. That responsibility
remains in the hands of God.

You may be called to a planting ministry for a period of
time. You may leave and someone else comes along and
waters. And perhaps someone else will reap, because
God gives the increase.

Some are reaping now. Someone else planted, perhaps in
tears for a long time. Some of you have prayer partners.
You know some of these elderly saints that are perhaps
bed-ridden and have been praying for your work for many
years. They have been watering with tears the seed that
someone else planted. Now you come along and maybe
you are beginning to see some fruit. God has given that
increase. It isn't you. You know that and I know that. We
are all partners together in what God has given. We are
fellow-laborers together with God—the one who plants,
the one who waters, and the one who has the joy of
reaping.

We all know that in the final analysis, it is God who does
the work. He says, "I am responsible for this. Jeremiah, I
started this whole thing. Before you were born, I knew
you. Before you were born, I consecrated you and
appointed you to be a prophet. And, therefore, Jeremiah, I
am not letting go now. I am watching over my word to
perform it."

As a college student, I believed for several years that
God was leading me to the land of Afghanistan. God did not
lead me there, and I never even saw that land until 1974. I
shall never forget the feeling as I looked out the window
of the plane as we flew in over that land where the gospel
has never been given with any freedom whatsoever and
where there is no national church. Coming into Kabul, the
capital city, I looked out on those little villages of

41

Afghanistan, knowing that in every village I could see, there is no established church that an Afghan can attend.

The next day, friends took me 200 miles up into the mountains to visit a remote place. We went through village after village, and I knew that there was no church in any of those villages. I also knew that over the years, many people of God have been watering that land with their prayers and with their tears, knowing that somehow, sometime God is going to do His work.

Recently I ran across an old issue of *His* magazine dated July 1946. I remembered this issue from my college days because it made a great impact on me. On the cover was a map of Afghanistan with a wall all the way around it. The articles inside talked about that walled-up land and how there was no missionary there at all giving the gospel. Those walls are still there. There are a few Christians in the land now, but no Afghan church.

The church of Jesus Christ exists today in almost every land of the world, but it doesn't exist in Afghanistan in any organized form. There is a church there, but it is for foreigners, not for Afghans. I preached in that church in January 1974. There were about 120 people present, but they were Germans, Norwegians, Indians, English, Dutch, Americans, and Canadians who were there in business and the diplomatic corps. There wasn't one Afghan in the meeting. It is against the law for an Afghan to go to such a church. It is still a law of the land that anyone who becomes a Christian can be put to death. So that land is closed up and one is tempted to ask, "Has God forgotten all about that land? Is nothing ever going to happen there?" But God says, "I am watching over my word to perform it. I haven't forgotten. I am the Alpha, but I am also the Omega. And I who began this and I who called you before

you were born am also the one who is going to carry it out. I
will complete my work."

Don't get discouraged. You never know what you
may be doing right now that is going to bear fruit later on.
Dr. J. Christy Wilson worked for more than twenty years in
Afghanistan and ended up being expelled from the
country. Yet Christy Wilson knows that God is doing
His work.

You may feel at times that God has forgotten all about
your particular little corner of His vineyard, since nothing
is happening there. Don't feel that way. God knows
what He is doing. Maybe you have been called to plant,
someone else is going to water, but it is only God that can
give the growth.

When I served on Inter-Varsity staff right after
graduation, before going to the mission field, I traveled all
over the country. I was much too young (I felt) for the job.
There were times when I got discouraged and wondered if
my work was bringing any results at all.

Recently I went into the mission headquarters of
Overseas Crusades in Palo Alto, California, to visit some of
my friends there. I was introduced to one man who said,
"Well, Dave Howard! I am surely glad to meet you. I
have been hearing about you for years."

"Through whom?"

He mentioned a name that rang no bell with me. He said,
"Do you know him?"

I said, "No."

"I worked with him in the Orient for fifteen years with
Overseas Crusades."

"Who is he?"

"Well," he said, "back when he was a student at Central
Washington University, you visited that campus for one

night. Apparently God used you somehow to turn his whole life around. He was headed in one direction but God turned his life completely around, and he has been a missionary in the Orient for fifteen years."

I never knew it. I wouldn't even recognize the fellow if I saw him on the street. I don't even remember his name now. But somehow that night some seed was planted that God used to change the whole life of a man.

This is one of those little words of encouragement that occasionally God gives to let us know that what we are doing is going to bear fruit even though we may never see it.

God says, "If I call you to be a prophet for Me, I will give you My words, I will give you My authority, and I will watch over My word to perform it."

PART TWO

The Ministry of Jeremiah

Then the Lord put forth his hand and touched my mouth; and the Lord said to me, "Behold, I have put my words in your mouth. See, I have set you this day over nations and over kingdoms, to pluck up and to break down, to destroy and to overthrow, to build and to plant."

And the word of the Lord came to me, saying, "Jeremiah, what do you see?" And I said, "I see a rod of almond." Then the Lord said to me, "You have seen well, for I am watching over my word to perform it."

The word of the Lord came to me a second time, saying, "What do you see?" And I said, "I see a boiling pot, facing away from the north." Then the Lord said to me, "Out of the north evil shall break forth upon all the inhabitants of the land. For, lo, I am calling all the tribes of the kingdoms of the north, says the Lord; and they shall come and every one shall set his throne at the entrance of the gates of Jerusalem, against all its walls round about, and against all the cities of Judah. And I will utter my judgments against them, for all their wickedness in forsaking me; they have burned incense to other gods, and worshiped the works of their own hands. But you, gird up your loins; arise, and say to them everything that I command you. Do not be dismayed by them, lest I dismay you before them. And I, behold, I make you this day a fortified city, an iron pillar, and bronze walls, against the whole land, against the kings of Judah, its princes, its priests, and the people of the land. They will fight against you; but they shall not prevail against you, for I am with you, says the Lord, to deliver you."

Jeremiah 1:9-19

CHAPTER FOUR

"The Best of Times, the Worst of Times"

The Setting for His Ministry

Charles Dickens opens *A Tale of Two Cities* with this famous paragraph:

> It was the best of times, it was the worst of times, it was the age of wisdom, it was the age of foolishness, it was the epic of belief, it was the epic of incredulity, it was the season of Light, it was the season of Darkness, it was the spring of hope, it was the winter of despair, we had everything before us, we had nothing before us, we were all going direct to Heaven, we were all going direct the other way....[1]

That pretty well describes the situation in Israel in the time of Jeremiah. It was the best of times, and it was the worst of times. Moving chronologically, it went from the

[1]Dickens, Charles, *A Tale of Two Cities* (New York: Collier Books, 1962), p. 19.

47

best to the worst. The opening verses of Jeremiah indicate when he was ministering.

> The words of Jeremiah, the son of Hilkiah, of the priests who were in Anathoth in the land of Benjamin, to whom the word of the Lord came in the days of Josiah the son of Amon, king of Judah, in the thirteenth year of his reign. It came also in the days of Jehoiakim the son of Josiah, king of Judah, and until the end of the eleventh year of Zedekiah, the son of Josiah, a king of Judah, until the captivity of Jerusalem in the fifth month. (Jeremiah 1:1-3)

The books of Kings and Chronicles describe what was happening during this period of time, first in the days of Josiah and then under the kings that followed him—Jehoahaz, Jehoiakim, Jehoiachin, and Zedekiah.

Jeremiah began ministering in the thirteenth year of the reign of Josiah. In 2 Kings 22 we find the beginnings of that king's reign. He was eight years old when he began to reign, and he reigned for thirty-one years in Jerusalem. 2 Kings 22:3, 4 says:

> In the eighteenth year of King Josiah, the king sent Shaphan the son of Azaliah, son of Meshullam, the secretary, to the house of the Lord, saying, "Go up to Hilkiah the high priest...."

This is five years after Jeremiah began his ministry, since he began in the thirteenth year of Josiah's reign. Jeremiah is, therefore, on the scene when this story takes place.

Josiah commands them to start cleaning up the house of the Lord. In the process of cleaning and rebuilding the house, Hilkiah, the high priest, comes across a book.

48

"I have found the book of the law in the house of the Lord." And Hilkiah gave the book to Shaphan, and he read it. And Shaphan the secretary came to the king.... (2 Kings 22:8, 9)

When the king saw this book of the law (which had apparently been lost for many years) in the house of the Lord, he was astounded at what he read. As he read it, he became impressed that this was the Word of God for all of Israel.

Then the king sent, and all the elders of Judah and Jerusalem were gathered to him. And the king went up to the house of the Lord, and with him all the men of Judah and all the inhabitants of Jerusalem, and the priests and the prophets, all the people, both small and great; and he read in their hearing all the words of the book of the covenant which had been found in the house of the Lord. And the king stood by the pillar and made a covenant before the Lord, to walk after the Lord and to keep his commandments and his testimonies and his statutes, with all his heart and all his soul, to perform the words of this covenant that were written in this book; and all the people joined in the covenant. (2 Kings 23:1-3)

It was a great time for Israel. Jeremiah was probably standing right there as this happened, because we read that all the prophets were there. Jeremiah listens as Josiah reads the book of the law, and they make their great covenant with God. Then Jeremiah watches as Josiah begins to put into practice what he has been commanded. Look at what Josiah does (2 Kings 22:4-24).

49

He took all the vessels that had been made for Baal and burned them outside Jerusalem. He deposed the idolatrous priests. He brought out the Asherah from the house of the Lord and burned it at the brook Kidron and beat it to dust. He broke down the houses of the male cult prostitutes. He defiled the high places, where false gods were worshiped. He defiled Topheth. He removed the horses that the kings of Judah had dedicated to the sun, and burned the chariots of the sun with fire. He pulled down the altars of the roof and broke them in pieces. He broke the pillars into pieces and cut down the Asherim. He pulled down the altar at Bethel and broke its stones into pieces. He took the bones out of the tombs and burned them upon the altar and defiled it, according to the word of the Lord. Josiah removed all the shrines and eliminated all the priests of the high places.

That was a pretty thorough job of cleaning out the Temple!

In obedience to God he kept the Passover.

> And the king commanded all the people, "Keep the passover to the Lord your God, as it is written in this book of the covenant." For no such passover had been kept since the days of the judges who judged Israel, or during all the days of the kings of Israel or of the kings of Judah; but in the eighteenth year of King Josiah this passover was kept to the Lord in Jerusalem. (2 Kings 23:21-23)

So Jeremiah watched and participated as for the first time in centuries, they kept the Passover according to the word of the Lord.

> Moreover Josiah put away the mediums and the wizards and the teraphim and the idols and all the

50

abominations that were seen in the land of Judah and in Jerusalem, that he might establish the words of the law which were written in the book that Hilkiah the priest found in the house of the Lord. (2 Kings 23:24)

He was ruthless in his war with idolatry, spiritism, and evil worship of any sort.

And finally, the summary about Josiah is this:

Before him there was no king like him, who turned to the Lord with all his heart and with all his soul and with all his might, according to all the law of Moses; nor did any like him arise after him. (2 Kings 23:25)

Josiah was the greatest king of Israel apart from David, who is set in another category. Of all the kings since the division of the kingdom between Israel and Judah, Josiah is clearly the one who stands out. So, in a sense, "It was the best of times." Jeremiah was there and saw all of this happening. He must have wondered in his heart what was going to happen in Israel, because he was already under the pressure of the word of the Lord announcing the coming judgment. Yet he saw this great revival in progress.

Unfortunately, Josiah didn't last too long. He did reign thirty-one years, but then he was killed by Pharaoh Neco of Egypt at the battle of Megiddo, and Jehoahaz his son mounted the throne. He reigned for three months and did that which was evil in the sight of the Lord.

Then Jehoiakim replaced him. He reigned for eleven years and was worse. Then Jehoiachin reigned for three months and he, too, was evil. And finally Zedekiah reigned for the final eleven years before the fall of Jerusalem. "And he did what was evil in the sight of the Lord..." (2 Kings 24:19).

So Jeremiah watched Israel plummet from a great peak of revival into the depths of the worst conceivable kind of sin. It should be noted that Jeremiah was probably born during the reign of Manasseh and had seen the evil and sinfulness that had characterized that period. So it must have been a doubly exciting thing for him to see the revival that took place under Josiah. Unfortunately, that revival didn't last. It wasn't long before Israel was living in the very worst of times.

CHAPTER FIVE

"The Supreme Prophet of the Human Heart"

The Content of His Ministry

Jeremiah is called upon by God in the thirteenth year of the reign of Josiah to start ministering. We don't know exactly when all of the messages came to him. Some of them are pinpointed to indicate the exact year, but others are not. It is well to note that the book of Jeremiah is not organized in chronological sequence. Any attempt to read it this way will result in confusion for the reader. Rather, it is organized topically, with prophecies and incidents placed at random as far as chronology is concerned.

What was it that Jeremiah spoke about? Alexander Whyte, in his book *Bible Characters,* says:

> Jeremiah was, of all the prophets of the Old Testament, the supreme prophet of the human heart ... Jeremiah would have nothing from his hearers and readers but their hearts. Let other prophets negotiate and send embassies as they

pleased. Jeremiah, in season and out of season, for a long lifetime laid siege to the heart of his hearers. The cure of all your diseases and all your plagues, he cried, and all your defeats and all your captivities—the cause and cure of them all is in your own heart: ... He who has—I will not say a full sensibility of the evil of sin, for he would go mad if he had—but a true beginning of such sensibility, he has the making of a true minister of Jesus Christ in him.[1]

In other words, the man who can comprehend something of the sinfulness of the human heart has the beginnings of the making of a true minister. "Speak to your hearer's heart and you will soon undermine his head," says Whyte.

Then Whyte exhorts young preachers, "Young preachers with your great life still before you, study your own heart day and night."[2]

Know what is going on in your own heart and you will be able to empathize a little better as you try to reach the hearts of those to whom you are ministering.

So Jeremiah was, of all the prophets of the Old Testament, the supreme prophet of the human heart. He knew what it was to look into his own heart and see his own sinfulness. Because of that, he could empathize with the terrible sinfulness of his people Israel.

What did he have to say to them? In the first chapter of his prophecy, dealing with the call of Jeremiah, we catch

---

[1]Whyte, Alexander, *Bible Characters* (Grand Rapids: Zondervan Publishing House, 1952), Vol. I, pp. 396, 397.
[2]*Ibid.*

a brief glimpse of what the content of his ministry was going to be. After the Lord told him in verse 9, "Behold, I have put my words in your mouth," he then said:

> "See, I have set you this day over nations and over kingdoms, to pluck up and to break down, to destroy and to overthrow, to build and to plant." (Jeremiah 1:10)

He was to announce judgment, "to pluck up and to break down, to destroy and to overthrow..." That was the negative aspect of his preaching. Much of Jeremiah's ministry was given to that. He had to denounce the sinfulness of Israel. He had to announce judgment.

Such preaching isn't very popular today. We tend to make fun of the old "hell-fire and brimstone" preachers who proclaim judgment. Yet it is very biblical. It is much more popular today to talk about sin in various euphemisms rather than to call it straightforward sin. It is easier to get into the psychological approach and analyze things as "shortcomings" or whatever else may be inoffensive, avoiding the judgmental aspects of sin. But the Word of God really gives us no other choice. Jeremiah had no choice. God's calling upon Jeremiah was, "You are to stand up and announce judgment; you are to pluck up and break down and destroy and overthrow." And he did just that. A great deal of the book of Jeremiah is given to that kind of preaching.

Jeremiah 25 is illustrative of this.

> "Therefore thus says the Lord of hosts: Because you have not obeyed my words, behold, I will send for all the tribes of the north, says the Lord, and for Nebuchadrezzar the king of Babylon, my servant, and I will bring them against this land and

its inhabitants, and against all these nations round about; I will utterly destroy them, and make them a horror, a hissing, and an everlasting reproach. Moreover, I will banish from them the voice of mirth and the voice of gladness, the voice of the bridegroom and the voice of the bride, the grinding of the millstones and the light of the lamp. This whole land shall become a ruin and a waste, and these nations shall serve the king of Babylon seventy years." (Jeremiah 25:8-11)

This is the announcement of impending judgment. Then notice this great oratory as it flows out eloquently declaring the coming doom.

"You, therefore, shall prophesy against them all these words, and say to them: 'The Lord will roar from on high, and from his holy habitation utter his voice; he will roar mightily against his fold, and shout, like those who tread grapes, against all the inhabitants of the earth. The clamor will resound to the ends of the earth, for the Lord has an indictment against the nations; he is entering into judgment with all flesh, and the wicked he will put to the sword, says the Lord.'

"Thus says the Lord of hosts: Behold, evil is going forth from nation to nation, and a great tempest is stirring from the farthest parts of the earth!

"And those slain by the Lord on that day shall extend from one end of the earth to the other. They shall not be lamented, or gathered, or buried; they shall be dung on the surface of the ground. Wail, you shepherds, and cry, and roll in ashes, you lords of the flock, for the days of your

slaughter and dispersion have come, and you shall
fall like choice rams. No refuge will remain for the
shepherds, nor escape for the lords of the flock.
Hark, the cry of the shepherds, and the wail of the
lords of the flock! For the Lord is despoiling their
pasture, and the peaceful folds are devastated,
because of the fierce anger of the Lord. Like a
lion he has left his covert, for their land has
become a waste because of the sword of the
oppressor, and because of his fierce anger."
(Jeremiah 25:30-38)

That is the Word of the Lord! You and I are called upon,
at times, to announce coming judgment. There is no way that
we can be faithful to God and avoid the judgmental
aspects of our ministry. We must recognize that sin
must be dealt with. It is impossible to be biblical and at the
same time sugar-coat the message of the gospel. The gospel
cuts right into the heart of man and into his sinfulness. As
Oswald Chambers has put it, "If there is no tragedy at
the back of human life, no gap between God and man,
then the Redemption of Jesus Christ is 'much ado about
nothing.' "[3]

Why was it that the Son of God Himself had to give His
very life? Because of the awfulness of sin. We can't get
away from that aspect of our message. When you and I
are called upon to minister for God, one part of our
message has to be to pluck up and to break down, to
overthrow and to destroy, to announce the coming
judgment of God against sin.

---

[3]Chambers, Oswald, *Baffled to Fight Better* (London: Marshall, Morgan & Scott, 1931),
p. 16.

57

Jeremiah's message did not end there. He was also
called upon to build and to plant. There was also the message
of mercy. Whenever God announces judgment, there is
always also the great truth that righteousness and peace
have met together. There is the merciful aspect of God.
Mercy and truth have kissed each other, because those two
things come together in the Cross of Jesus Christ. This
truth also is spread throughout the book of Jeremiah.
As you look through the book, you will find again and
again little glimpses—in the midst of awful judgment as
eloquent as the previous passage—where the great mercy
of God is announced. Notice Chapter 31 as an
illustration of the mercy which Jeremiah was preaching to
the people of Israel. Again it is very eloquent.

> "At that time, says the Lord, I will be the God of all
> the families of Israel, and they shall be my
> people." Thus says the Lord: "The people who
> survived the sword found grace in the wilderness;
> when Israel sought for rest, the Lord appeared to
> him from afar. I have loved you with an
> everlasting love; therefore I have continued my
> faithfulness to you. Again I will build you, and you
> shall be built, O virgin Israel! Again you shall
> adorn yourself with timbrels, and shall go forth
> in the dance of the merrymakers. Again you shall
> plant vineyards upon the mountains of Samaria; the
> planters shall plant, and shall enjoy the fruit. For
> there shall be a day when watchmen will call in
> the hill country of Ephraim: 'Arise, and let us go up
> to Zion, to the Lord our God.' " For thus says the
> Lord: "Sing aloud with gladness for Jacob, and
> raise shouts for the chief of the nations;

proclaim, give praise, and say, 'The Lord has saved
his people, the remnant of Israel.' Behold, I will bring
them from the north country, and gather them
from the farthest parts of the earth, among them
the blind and the lame, the woman with child and
her who is in travail, together; a great company, they
shall return here. With weeping they shall come,
and with consolations I will lead them back, I
will make them walk by brooks of water, in a
straight path in which they shall not stumble; for I am
a father to Israel, and Ephraim is my first-born."
(Jeremiah 31:1-9)

Here we see the beautiful, loving expression of a Father
to His people. The one who has just announced awful
judgment and that terrible outpouring in Jeremiah 25 and
other passages, is the same one who says in the midst of
all of this, "I am a father to Israel, and Ephraim is my
first-born son and I love you as a father loves you, with an
everlasting love. Therefore with lovingkindness—
everlasting lovingkindness—have I drawn you."
That's the heart of the message of the gospel. God
must judge sin. God must punish the terrible corruption
of His people. But at the same time, "I am a father to
Israel, and Ephraim is my first-born. I have loved you
with an everlasting love." Therefore, there comes a
message of mercy as well as of judgment.
Chapter 31 goes on:

Thus says the Lord: "Keep your voice from
weeping, and your eyes from tears; for your work
shall be rewarded, says the Lord, and they shall come
back from the land of the enemy. There is a hope
for your future, says the Lord, and your children

shall come back to their own country. I have heard
Ephraim bemoaning, 'Thou has chastened me, and I
was chastened, like an untrained calf; bring me
back that I may be restored, for thou art the
Lord my God. For after I had turned away I
repented; and after I was instructed, I smote upon my
thigh; I was ashamed, and I was confounded,
because I bore the disgrace of my youth.' Is
Ephraim my dear son? Is he my darling child? For
as often as I speak against him, I do remember him
still. Therefore my heart yearns for him; I will
surely have mercy on him, says the Lord."
(Jeremiah 31:16-20)

What a beautiful passage! "The very child I *must* punish
because of his sins, I still love. I am his father. I remember
him still. My heart yearns for him. I will surely have
mercy on him," says the Lord. All through the Old
Testament and all through the New Testament, there is that
thread of the mercy of God. It begins all the way back in
the Garden of Eden where God makes it clear that He
will find a way out from sin; that although sin must be
judged, He Himself is providing the ransom for that sin. All
Scripture vibrates with that great message of mercy.

You and I are called upon, in our ministry in
witnessing to others, to make clear the judgment of God
against sin and the mercy of God who has provided the way
out of that sin. Nowhere is this seen more clearly than in
the ministry of Jeremiah.

CHAPTER SIX

"I Sat Alone"
The Results of His Ministry

What did it cost Jeremiah to follow the Lord? What happened to Jeremiah because he obeyed God? It would be nice to teach younger Christians—and to be able to claim for ourselves—that when we commit ourselves to Jesus Christ and follow God, all of our problems are solved. I once heard a man make that statement from a platform to a large crowd of people. He said, "When you receive Jesus Christ, your problems are over." It would be great if that were true.

But you know, on the basis of your own experience and on the basis of Scripture, that such is not the case. God never promises that our problems are over once we commit ourselves to Jesus Christ. He does promise to provide grace in the wilderness. He does promise to provide the strength that we need. He does tell us that He is our loving Father and that He will sustain us with everlasting love. But that doesn't mean that the problems

end. Look at the life of Jeremiah. Here is a man who was
obedient to God, a man who could not keep quiet.
When God told him to speak, he spoke. And what
happened?

> Now Pashhur the priest, the son of Immer, who
> was chief officer in the house of the Lord, heard
> Jeremiah prophesying these things. Then Pashhur
> beat Jeremiah the prophet, and put him in the stocks
> that were in the upper Benjamin Gate of the house
> of the Lord. (Jeremiah 20:1, 2)

And there he sits in the stocks! He is in prison simply
because he did what God told him to do.

I remember years ago in Colombia meeting a man
named Alfredo who had become a Christian a few
months earlier. This was in a time when the evangelical
Christians were living under severe persecution. He lived in
an area where such persecution was common. One day he
was preaching the gospel in an open plaza. A local
ecclesiastical dignitary came along and asked, "What are
you doing here?"

"I am preaching the gospel."

"That's not your job, that's mine."

Alfredo replied, "If you were doing it, I wouldn't have
to."

The other man slapped him in the face, called the police,
and had him put into stocks right out in the middle of
the plaza. So here was Alfredo, a Christian for only six
months, sitting out in the middle of the plaza with his hands
and feet in stocks.

It happened to be a Sunday afternoon. That evening
Alfredo was scheduled to speak in the little evangelical
church in that village. So about 4:00 P.M. he called for the

mayor of the town. The mayor came out and said, "What's your problem?"

"Well," said Alfredo, "I need to get out of the stocks now, because I am scheduled to preach tonight here in the church."

The mayor said, "Oh, no. You are not getting out to preach."

"Well," he said, "if I don't, the congregation will come here to the plaza, and I will preach to them here."

The mayor thought that one over for a moment and decided that it would be more discreet to let him out and let him preach behind closed doors. So they released him, and he went and preached his message.

He told me about this a few weeks later with a great smile on his face. This is what it cost him to obey God. As he announced judgment and mercy, he suffered for it. But he was rejoicing that God had counted him worthy to suffer.

In Jeremiah 26:7-11 we read this:

> The priests and the prophets and all the people heard Jeremiah speaking these words in the house of the Lord. And when Jeremiah had finished speaking all that the Lord had commanded him to speak to all the people, then the priests and the prophets and all the people laid hold of him, saying, "You shall die! Why have you prophesied in the name of the Lord, saying, 'This house shall be like Shiloh, and this city shall be desolate, without inhabitant'?" And all the people gathered about Jeremiah in the house of the Lord.
>
> When the princes of Judah heard these things, they came up from the king's house to the house of the Lord and took their seat in the entry of the New

> Gate of the house of the Lord. Then the priests
> and the prophets said to the princes and to all
> the people, "This man deserves the sentence of
> death, because he has prophesied against this city, as
> you have heard with your own ears."

Jeremiah has already been in the stocks and now they
are threatening him with death. In Chapter 32 we find him
in prison again.

> At that time the army of the king of Babylon was
> besieging Jerusalem, and Jeremiah the prophet
> was shut up in the court of the guard which was in
> the palace of the king of Judah. (Jeremiah 32:2)

This is in the tenth year of Zedekiah, one year before
the fall of Jerusalem. Thus it is close to the end of
Jeremiah's ministry. He is an aging prophet by now.
He also had to live with the bitterness of false accusations.

> Now when the Chaldean army had withdrawn
> from Jerusalem at the approach of Pharaoh's
> army, Jeremiah set out from Jerusalem to go to the
> land of Benjamin to receive his portion there among
> the people. When he was at the Benjamin Gate, a
> sentry there named Irijah the son of Shelemiah,
> son of Hananiah, seized Jeremiah the prophet
> saying, "You are deserting to the Chaldeans." And
> Jeremiah said, "It is false; I am not deserting to the
> Chaldeans." But Irijah would not listen to him,
> and seized Jeremiah and brought him to the
> princes. And the princes were enraged at Jeremiah,
> and they beat him and imprisoned him in the
> house of Jonathan the secretary, for it had been
> made a prison. (Jeremiah 37:11-15)

It is one thing to be put in prison when you know you are wrong. But to be put in prison being accused of things that you never did must be doubly difficult. Jeremiah again was simply obeying God, and this brought beatings and imprisonment.

What we have spoken about up to this point have been the physical results of his ministry. What about the emotional results of his ministry?

Because he did what God told him to do, he was rejected by the people of his own town, Anathoth, which was about three miles from Jerusalem.

> Therefore thus says the Lord concerning the men of Anathoth, who seek your life, and say, "Do not prophesy in the name of the Lord, or you will die by our hand." (Jeremiah 11:21)

His own townspeople are threatening him with death. That must have been emotionally traumatic for him. These were his own people. These were the boys and girls that he grew up with on the streets. These are the ones that he used to play with as a child. Now they are telling him, "We are going to put you to death if you don't stop talking this way."

He was also rejected by the entire nation.

> The word that came to Jeremiah concerning all the people of Judah, in the fourth year of Jehoiakim the son of Josiah, king of Judah (that was the first year of Nebuchadrezzar king of Babylon), which Jeremiah the prophet spoke to all the people of Judah and all the inhabitants of Jerusalem: "For twenty-three years, from the thirteenth year of Josiah the son of Amon, king of Judah, to this day,

the word of the Lord has come to me, and I have
spoken persistently to you, but you have not
listened. You have neither listened nor inclined
your ears to hear, although the Lord persistently sent
to you all his servants the prophets, saying, 'Turn
now, every one of you, from his evil way and
wrong doings, and dwell upon the land which the
Lord has given to you and your fathers from of old
and for ever; do not go after other gods to serve
and worship them, or provoke me to anger with
the work of your hands. Then I will do you no
harm.' Yet you have not listened to me, says the
Lord, that you might provoke me to anger with the
work of your hands to your own harm."
(Jeremiah 25:1-7)

Jeremiah had now been preaching for twenty-three years
and the people would not listen. Have you begun to think
that people aren't listening to you? Supposing God asks
you to stay in one place for twenty-three years and nobody
listens? Would you be willing to stay? Imagine speaking to
them persistently, in the name of the Lord, with the words
that God put in your mouth, and all they did was slap
you and throw you in dungeons and put you in the stocks!
Would you be up to that for twenty-three years? When you
tend to feel discouraged over lack of results, take heart.
Look at Jeremiah. Things could be a lot worse!

He was also rejected by the king himself. He
occasionally got into the presence of the king and had direct
words for him. As he was dictating the words of God, his
secretary, Baruch, would write them down. Then a
young man named Jehudi would read these to the king.

Then the king sent Jehudi to get the scroll, and he

took it from the chamber of Elishama the
secretary; and Jehudi read it to the king and all
the princes who stood beside the king. It was the
ninth month, and the king was sitting in the winter
house and there was a fire burning in the brazier
before him. As Jehudi read three or four
columns, the king would cut them off with a
penknife and throw them into the fire in the brazier.
(Jeremiah 36:21-23)

That must have been rather discouraging. It takes a
long time to write out a scroll by hand. The king sat there
and listened to three or four columns. Then he took his
knife, chopped them up, and threw them into the fire.
That's my attitude towards the Word of God, he said.
Have you had people respond that way to you in their
attitude towards the Word of God? Think how discouraging
it would be when the king himself showed that kind of
attitude.

In our first years in Costa Rica, my wife and I lived in
Santo Domingo, a little town outside the city of San Jose.
Santo Domingo was a village where the gospel had never
taken root. There was one Christian family in the town
and a scattered number of three or four believers
elsewhere in the town. We used to meet with them regularly
on Sundays for worship and teaching. It was a very difficult
town, tightly closed to the gospel. Sometimes I would
join one of the believers going from door to door
distributing the Scriptures into the homes of these people. In
these days there were great tensions between Roman
Catholics and Protestants. It sometimes reached the
point of hatred. Many people had in their windows a sign
that said, *"Somos católicos, no aceptamos propaganda*

67

protestante," which means, "We are Catholics, we do not accept Protestant propaganda."

Sometimes we would go to the door of such houses and offer them a portion of a Scripture. The lady would say, "Don't you see that sign in my window?"

And we would reply, "But this isn't Protestant propaganda. This is the Word of God. We would like you to have the Word of God if you are willing to read it."

"You want to know what I think of that?" She would grab it out of our hand, tear it up in pieces, and throw it in our faces. "That is what I think of what you have to give to me."

That is a bit of what Jeremiah and his friends were facing. They would write it out, the king would chop it up with his penknife and throw it into the fire. It was total rejection of the Word of God.

Jeremiah must have had to face great emotional problems when this kind of thing would happen. He fell into the depths of despair at times.

> My grief is beyond healing, my heart is sick within me...For the wound of the daughter of my people is my heart wounded, I mourn, and dismay has taken hold on me. (Jeremiah 8:18, 21)

> O that I had in the desert a wayfarers' lodging place, that I might leave my people and go away from them! For they are all adulterers, a company of treacherous men. (Jeremiah 9:2)

Jeremiah is saying, "I wish I could run away from it all. I wish I could just get out of this whole business. I would like to run away from my people. They are all treacherous people. They are all adulterous men."

Have you ever felt that way in your work? You have a bad day, and everyone seems to be against you. Things go from bad to worse, and by ten o'clock that night you retreat to your room absolutely discouraged. You want to say, "I want to get away from it all. I never want to see that place again. I want to run away." That is exactly what Jeremiah was going through. Things are getting too tough for me. Twenty-three years of this! I would like to get out of it all. I wish I could get away.

He even despairs of his own life.

> Cursed be the day on which I was born! The day when my mother bore me, let it not be blessed! Cursed be the man who brought the news to my father, "A son is born to you," making him very glad. Let that man be like the cities which the Lord overthrew without pity; let him hear a cry in the morning and an alarm at noon, because he did not kill me in the womb; so my mother would have been my grave, and her womb for ever great. Why did I come forth from the womb to see toil and sorrow, and spend my days in shame?
> (Jeremiah 20:14-18)

It is the depths of despair when a person cries out, "I wish I had never been born. I wish I had never seen the light of day."

Recently I was talking with a young student who told me that he had almost reached that place himself. He said, "A few weeks ago I got to the place where I was asking God to take my life. I wasn't thinking of taking my own life but I asked God to take it. It was just too much. I wanted to get away from everything. I had had enough. So I wanted God to take me away."

69

If you feel that way occasionally, remember that Jeremiah did too. Jeremiah cursed his birthday and never wanted to hear of it again.

Then there are those tears that flowed so freely, causing him to be called the "weeping prophet."

> O that my head were waters, and my eyes a fountain of tears, that I might weep day and night for the slain of the daughter of my people! (Jeremiah 9:1)

> But if you will not listen, my soul will weep in secret for your pride; my eyes will weep bitterly and run down with tears, because the Lord's flock has been taken captive. (Jeremiah 13:17)

How many of us know what it really means to weep over the sins of other people? Jeremiah is famous as the "weeping prophet." But why was he the "weeping prophet?" Because he was the prophet to the heart of his people. Because he identified with his people and saw the awfulness of sin and the fearful judgment of God. He loved his people. So he wept because he saw what was going to happen to them if they did not repent.

The weeping of Jeremiah was not for his own suffering. When he was in prison, we don't find him weeping for himself. When he was beaten and thrown into the cistern, we don't find him weeping for his own problem. He was weeping because of the sinfulness of his people.

Even that weeping didn't change things, although it helped Jeremiah himself in a sense. Alexander Whyte makes this comment about the tears of Jeremiah:

> Tears, when bitter enough and in secret enough, will always gain forgiveness. But while such tears will

70

always avail under grace to blot out the past, they
have no power to bring back the past. Nor do
they bring in the sure future, so much as one day,
before its time. All Jeremiah's tears did not keep back
the Chaldeans for a single day's march. But his
tears softened his heart and bowed his head.[1]

Jeremiah's tears didn't stop Nebuchadnezzar from
coming into Jerusalem, but they softened his own heart in his
relationship to God. His tears made him tender to other
people. His tears made him sensitive to God.

Neither his tears nor his prayers nor his
resignations nor his submissions shortened by a
single hour the seventy years captivity, but his
tears did far better for himself at least. They
perfected what both nature and grace so well
began. For they made him not only an evangelical
prophet but almost a New Testament apostle.[2]

Jeremiah's tears didn't change the course of history.
But they softened his heart and made him a man after
God's own heart. They almost made him a New Testament
apostle in his understanding of grace, because he
understood something of what true forgiveness was
going to mean.
    So there was a place for tears in the ministry of Jeremiah,
and there can be a place for tears in our ministry. If you
and I know nothing at all of tears, maybe we should ask
God to soften our hearts that we might understand better
the depth of sin and the coming judgment. Then perhaps we

---

[1]Whyte, *op. cit.*, Vol. I, p. 399.
[2]*Ibid.*

could empathize better with those who are going to be judged unless the mercy and forgiveness of God reaches them.

Jeremiah also suffered desperate loneliness. There is a very significant little phrase tucked away in Chapter 15 in the middle of another long passage.

> I did not sit in the company of merrymakers, nor did I rejoice; I sat alone, because thy hand was upon me... (Jeremiah 15:17)

"I could not participate with the merrymakers and with the others. There were things that I could not do because the hand of God was upon me." Do you know what it is to be lonely because the hand of God is upon you? Do you know what it is not to be able to participate in things that might be perfectly legitimate but you know that the hand of God is upon you? There will be times when you must sit absolutely alone because God has called you to Himself and asked you to do a job.

Some of you may be entirely alone in the work God has given you. You may not see another Christian worker as often as you would like. You may not have found a really close prayer partner. You may have to sit there and say, "Lord, I am sitting alone because your hand is upon me. I came to this task because you laid your hand upon me for this. But the result is that I have to sit alone today."

That loneliness of having responded to the call of God is something which every one of us sooner or later may have to experience. When it comes, don't take it as any great exceptional thing. Don't take it as any great surprise. God may be laying His hand upon you and you have to stand alone for a period of time. God may, in His graciousness, provide that companionship, that help, and that

72

encouragement through others that you need. But don't be surprised when loneliness sets in.

In 1956, when Jim Elliot and his four friends were killed by the Auca Indians, I went to Ecuador from Costa Rica to be with my sister Elisabeth, Jim's widow. I spent about two weeks with her following Jim's death. I returned with her to Shandia where she and Jim had been working among the Quicha Indians. I stayed in the home that Jim had built with his own hands and tried to help Elisabeth get reorganized by doing a little work around the place for her.

Then the time came when I had to go back to my family in Costa Rica. Elisabeth was the only foreigner left in Ecuador who knew the language of that particular group of Indians in the jungles. Three of the five men had known the language. One of the wives had known it, but she was returning to the States to have a child. Elisabeth was thus the only missionary left who could minister to the Quicha Indians in their language. There were very few believers in that tribe.

I remember taking off in the Mission Aviation Fellowship plane leaving Shandia, and looking back into that little clearing and out over that vast, green expanse of the jungle. As we flew away, I could see Elisabeth standing in that clearing entirely alone. Here was a person who, because it was at that time God's will for her, had to stay absolutely alone. There was no other way.

I remember hearing Elisabeth asking spiritual counselors who could help her at that time, "What am I going to do? What can I do?" One older, very godly man said to her, "Elisabeth, you have no choice. You are the only person left who speaks the language of these people, and you can't stand on ceremony and say, 'But I'm a woman. I can't

73

speak.' You know the language and you have got to speak. Now you stay there and teach them the Word of God." And so she stood there in that little clearing, and I flew off. I remember thinking, "Of all the lonely places I have ever seen in my life, that's the loneliest." But God was with her. God may want you to say, with Jeremiah, "I sat alone, because thy hand was upon me."

When Elisabeth was in college, she wrote the following poem, not fully realizing at the time how truly prophetic it was:

> Perhaps some future day, Lord, Thy
>   strong hand
> Will lead me to the place where I must
>   stand
>   Utterly alone.
>
> Alone, O gracious Lover, but for Thee.
> I shall be satisfied if I can see
>   Jesus only.
>
> I do not know Thy plan for years to come,
> My spirit finds in Thee its perfect home,
>   Sufficiency.
>
> Lord, all my desire is before Thee now;
> Lead on—no matter where, no matter
>   how,
>   I trust in Thee.

That loneliness may be aggravated by something else that happened to Jeremiah. Look at Chapter 16. There is no explanation of this factor, but rather just a simple statement of fact. If you consider the depths of the implications of this, you may get the picture a little more clearly.

> The word of the Lord came to me: "You shall not
> take a wife, nor shall you have sons or daughters in
> this place." (Jeremiah 16:1, 2)

Jeremiah was not allowed to marry, because of God's
demands upon him. In over forty years of a long ministry,
Jeremiah never experienced the joy of having a wife to
share these trials with him. He never had the joy of a
home life. He never knew what it was to have little
children playing around his feet. He did not know the
laughter of children in his home. He did not know the
comfort and compassion of a wife. When he would
come home from preaching in the Temple or in the king's
palace, having been beaten and rejected, he had no wife to go
home to, no one to whom he could pour out his sorrows.
Why God did not permit this is not entirely clear. But
God does indicate to him that "I have my hand upon you
and I must become to you all that human companionship
would be."

Jeremiah had almost no friends, though there were
one or two men mentioned by name that helped him out.
Baruch was apparently a close friend. Ebedmelech was the
man who hauled him out of the cistern. But outside of one
or two men like that, he had almost no friends and he
had no wife.

Those whom God calls to a single life will have to go
through life learning what it was that Jeremiah went
through. I have been happily married since I was
twenty-two and, therefore, cannot fully empathize with
those who have not been allowed by God to have that
particular relationship in life. But God's plans for some
will be that. Are you willing that the hand of God should
be upon you and not allow you that particular area of life?

THE MINISTRY OF JEREMIAH

Sometimes it is because God has called to a specific
ministry. Barbara Boyd is a woman who has had a
wonderful ministry over the years because God has used
her as a single woman. Barbara has been God's instrument in
building the whole Bible and Life movement (a branch of
Inter-Varsity Christian Fellowship). God has touched
thousands of lives around this country through her. She
has done something that she could not have done had she
been married.

There was a time when Barbara was planning to be
married. I knew her fiancé, Ralph Willoughby, an
Inter-Varsity staff member. After several years on IV staff,
he went to Fuller Seminary. On his way back East
following graduation from Fuller, God chose to take
him home in a sudden and unexpected way. God took
from Barbara that joy of life which she had been anticipating.
The result was that she has gone on through life in a single
state and has had a great ministry because of that.

Are you willing to face up to the implications of that? In
God's inscrutable and sovereign ways, He may lay His hand
upon you for a ministry for which He asks you to remain
single. This is God's way. It was His way with Jeremiah.

Finally, at the end of his life, Jeremiah was forced to do
something that he didn't want to do. In Chapter 43 he was
taken down to Egypt. He said, "I have to stay here in
Jerusalem." They said, "No, you are coming to Egypt
with us." The Israelites forced him to go to Egypt against
his own will. There is no indication that Jeremiah ever
returned to Jerusalem. In fact, tradition says that he died
in Egypt. One tradition indicates that he was put to
death by the Jews themselves, perhaps by being sawed in
two.

So how did he end a long life of faithful ministry for

God? He ended it in shame and despair, taken off to a foreign land, and probably put to death by the hands of his own people. This is what it cost Jeremiah to follow God. Are you willing to follow God at such a cost?

Most of us—sooner or later in life—are allowed some encouragement. To most of us, God gives the companionship that we need. He gives us some results. But some are called upon to face a long life of service with no tangible results.

Ernest Fowler, one of my closest colleagues in Colombia, spent thirty-two years trying to reach one tribe of Indians with the gospel. In his first attempt to reach that tribe, he was literally driven out by satanic forces. The second time he tried, he was driven out by persecution. On his third attempt he was murdered and buried in the high Andes Mountains of Colombia. His body lies today in a shallow grave that was dug by his children and my son, who were with him at that time. At the time of his death, there were almost no visible results of the work that he tried for thirty-two years to establish. That was the end of Ernest Fowler's life, a life similar to Jeremiah's. He was a man who faithfully preached the Word of God and yet saw no great results.

There is more to the book of Jeremiah that is more positive. But one cannot read the book without seeing the negative as well. It is there. We have to reckon with it. This is part of the cost of following the Lord.

> No one who puts his hand to the plow and looks back is fit for the kingdom of God. (Luke 9:62)

> For which of you, desiring to build a tower, does not first sit down and count the cost, whether he has enough to complete it? (Luke 14:28)

77

Margaret Clarkson has written a hymn which reflects something of the truth of Jeremiah. It says:

> So send I you to labor unrewarded,
> To serve unpaid, unloved, unsought, unknown;
> To bear rebuke, to suffer scorn and scoffing.
> So send I you, to toil for me alone.
>
> So send I you to bind the bruised and broken,
> O'er wandering souls to work, to weep, to wake;
> To bear the burdens of a world aweary.
> So send I you to suffer for my sake.
>
> So send I you to loneliness and longing;
> With heart a hungering for the loved and known;
> Forsaking home and kindred, friend and dear one.
> So send I you to know my love alone.
>
> As the Father has sent me, so send I you.

PART THREE

The Hope of Jeremiah

*Thus says the Lord: "Cursed is the man who
trusts in man and makes flesh his arm, whose
heart turns away from the Lord. He is like a
shrub in the desert, and shall not see any good
come. He shall dwell in the parched places of the
wilderness, in an uninhabited salt land.
Blessed is the man who trusts in the Lord,
whose trust is the Lord. He is like a tree
planted by water, that sends out its roots by the
stream, and does not fear when heat comes, for
its leaves remain green, and is not anxious
in the year of drought, for it does not cease to
bear fruit." The heart is deceitful above all
things, and desperately corrupt; who can
understand it? "I the Lord search the mind
and try the heart, to give to every man
according to his ways, according to the fruit of his
doings." Like the partridge that gathers a
brood which she did not hatch, so is he who
gets riches but not by right; in the midst of his
days they will leave him, and at his end he will be*

79

a fool. A glorious throne set on high from the beginning is the place of our sanctuary. O Lord, the hope of Israel, all who forsake thee shall be put to shame; those who turn away from thee shall be written in the earth, for they have forsaken the Lord, the fountain of living water.

Jeremiah 17:5-13

CHAPTER SEVEN

"Cursed Is the Man Who Trusts in Man"

The Dangers of Fleshly Effort

In this passage there is, first of all, a curse, then a blessing, then a warning, and finally a solution. We will examine these as we consider the hope which Jeremiah had in the midst of almost continual setbacks and despair.

> ...Cursed is the man who trusts in man and makes flesh his arm, whose heart turns away from the Lord. (Jeremiah 17:5)

What does it mean to trust in man? Jeremiah expands this by saying, "He makes flesh his arm [and his] heart turns away from the Lord."

Now if I were to ask you as a Christian if you are trusting in man, I am sure you would answer, "No, I am trusting in the Lord."

But is it possible for us as Christians to trust in man instead of the Lord? We would say, "I am not letting my heart turn away from the Lord. I am not turning to the flesh." But is that true? Is it not possible from time to time, without realizing it, to be trusting in man more than we are trusting in the Lord?

What goes on in our minds when we are talking with others about the Lord, whether it be talking with a Christian or with a non-Christian? Am I thinking, perhaps subconsciously, that my words are going to get through to him better than God's Word?

Some years ago I was speaking on the campus of a Christian college. One of the professors who had been there for many years took me aside one day and said, "I would like to help you understand this campus a little better." She gave me some valuable time to give me insights into the students. The campus, according to her, was going through a period of great turmoil. The students were turned off by traditional Christianity. They were characterized by cynicism and reaction. Many of them had come out of Christian homes but felt that they had to rebel to show their own independence.

After giving me a general survey of current attitudes, the professor said, "Dave, I have to stay twenty miles away from the Bible when I talk to these students so that I don't turn them off." And I thought, "What a tragic situation!"—tragic for her even more than for the students. Whether she realized it or not (and I don't think she did), she was saying, "My words will get through to them better than God's Word."

Let's not fall into that trap. It is a very easy one for Christian workers to fall into, feeling that *my* words to these students will get through better than the Word of God.

You will encounter people who say, "I don't accept the Bible as the Word of God." That doesn't change the fact that it still is the Word of God. It is quick and powerful and sharper than any two-edged sword. It will divide and cut right into the heart of man. Whether they accept it as the Word of God is not the basic issue. Their attitude towards the Bible has nothing to do with whether or not you and I ought to use the Word of God. When we talk to someone like that, we may tend to think, "He doesn't accept the Bible. Therefore, I have to stay away from the Scripture until he is willing to accept the Bible. Then maybe I can use it." No! That is trusting in man rather than trusting in God. Jeremiah says, "Cursed is the man who trusts in man and makes flesh his arm."

There are other areas where we as Christians can trust in man without realizing it. It can be a very subtle kind of thing. At this point I am going to tread on some dangerous ground. I wish to refer to a "sacred cow" which I realize is very much honored today, but about which I have some concern. Sharing in small groups has been widely accepted in recent years. Without a doubt, God has wonderfully used this in the lives of many of us. There is not a thing in the world wrong with a small group sharing together, unless that small group begins to depend on itself rather than on the Word of God. And strangely enough, this can happen. We sit down together and share where we each find ourselves right now. I'll tell you where I hurt and where I am. Where do you hurt? That is a great starter and can be a means of leading on to our growth. But if we just continue sharing without getting around to objective, biblical solutions to our problems, pretty soon it becomes nothing more than a mingling of your ignorance with my ignorance.

I was with a group of people at a summer conference who came from a church in the Midwest where they practiced this sharing concept. They were a tightly knit group.

They were young married couples, mostly in their twenties and thirties. There were both Christians and non-Christians in the group as far as I could discern. They invited me into their fellowship several times during the week in the late evening, after the evening services.

At the end of the week, one of them said to me, "We don't know what we are going to do when we go back to our church."

"I said, "Why?"

"Well, the problem is that we all know each other so well, we all know what the other one is going to say. We don't have anything left to say to each other. We have said everything there is to say."

My reaction was, "Did it ever occur to you to find out what God has to say to you? Have you thought about opening the Bible and listening to God? You haven't exhausted that yet, have you? You may have exhausted what you know about each other, and you may be able to predict what the other one is going to say, but what about God's Word to you?"

When the small group concept gets to the place where we do so much sharing of each other that we are subtly drawn away from digging into what the Word of God has to say, then we are in trouble. That is one way of trusting in man or trusting in the flesh. Jeremiah warns us strongly about that.

There is also the danger of confidence in activity. Activity does not automatically bring spirituality. We know that in our mind. Yet as we evaluate our efforts to serve the Lord, it is easy to equate activity with spirituality. We may tend to take our spiritual temperature by saying: "I have talked to so many Christians about their needs. I have witnessed to so many non-Christians. But last month

I witnessed to twice as many non-Christians, so I am not as spiritual this month as I was last month."

While this may be an accurate diagnosis of our spiritual state under some circumstances, it is not necessarily true. The amount of activity doesn't always show one's spiritual development.

Now there are times when a declining state is clearly evident by a lack of activity on our part. But the two things are not necessarily synonymous. The fact that I am doing more one particular week than another is no guarantee that I am, therefore, closer to the Lord. This will be seen not only in our interpersonal relationships but also in our need for material things. Fund-raising for Christian work, for example, may demonstrate this.

A young missionary candidate is seeking support for going overseas. A church sees the unreached and needy multitudes in its own backyard and wants to expand its outreach to them in loving service. A mission sees great need and endless opportunities for outreach with the gospel to those who have never heard. A Christian organization sees the crying tragedy of famine and poverty in the world, and genuinely wants to help alleviate this. But all of this takes money. How should they go about it?

There are two opposite viewpoints on how to approach this. One is to say, "I will do nothing but pray about it." That may be the way that God would lead you to do it. Someone else takes the opposite approach and does nothing but work on fund-raising, possibly even neglecting his own prayer life in the rush of activity. Somewhere in between, others will seek the balance between faith and works.

I don't know how God will lead in your life in the area of finances. I don't suppose there are two Christian workers or missionaries with whom God has worked in exactly the same way in raising support. God will raise support for some in one way and for others another way. Just because someone else has a certain experience, that doesn't mean that this will be your experience.

Often when I speak to students about missions, they ask, "Will I have to raise my own support if I go out under a mission board?"

That is a problem with many students as you can well imagine.

Sometimes they ask, "How did you get your support?"

I don't even like to tell them, because in our case the Lord worked in a way that won't be duplicated with many others. I didn't have to go through some of the struggles that many young people face in raising support. I have seen some candidates heading for the mission field who spent two years trying to raise their support. And some have never gotten there because they haven't been able to get their support. That is the way God deals with some. He may be testing you along certain lines. So don't take someone else's experiences as your standard. Don't look at someone else and say, "God dealt with him that way and, therefore, He is going to deal with me that same way." No, that is trusting in the flesh rather than trusting in the Lord.

What you have to find out is, "God, what do You want to teach me in this situation? Why am I having such a hard time with the area of finance when someone else had such an easy time? How am I to be growing in this situation? What do You want me to learn so that I won't be trusting in the flesh, trying to copy someone else, rather than learning what You plan to teach me in the midst of this?"

Thus you are turning away from trusting in the flesh

and learning to trust in the Lord.

Now what are the results for the man who trusts in the flesh?

> He is like a shrub in the desert, and shall not see any good come. He shall dwell in the parched places of the wilderness, in an uninhabited salt land.
> (Jeremiah 17:6)

This is a picture of absolute barrenness. The man who is trusting in the flesh is a barren person.

Years ago I heard Dr. T. J. Bach, who was then the General Director of The Evangelical Alliance Mission, say, "Beware the barrenness of a busy life." There are few greater dangers for a Christian worker than that. Every Christian worker (so-called "full-time" or otherwise) knows what it is to be busy. There is always more work than one can possibly do. There are more non-Christians to reach, more needy people to help, more Christians to encourage, more fellow-workers to support than anyone can cope with. The tendency is to become so active, trusting in the flesh, that soon the barrenness of a busy life begins to set in and "he [becomes] like a shrub in the desert, and shall not see any good come. He shall dwell in the parched places of the wilderness, in an uninhabited salt land." We need to be reminded again that fleshly activity is not to be equated with spirituality.

I have this temptation as much as anyone. I know something of the barrenness of a busy life. While in college I used to think that it would be easier when I got out of college to have a quiet time, because then I would be able to set my own schedules. Quite the opposite has been true. It was much easier in college days when I had a schedule to follow and had to go to class at a given hour. I

have had more problems with quiet time in the years since
college than I ever did during those days.

I used to think, "When I become a missionary, I will
have to have a quiet time, so there won't be any problem." I
had a rude awakening coming! I had to learn the hard way
the truth of the old adage that crossing an ocean doesn't
make a missionary—nor does it make having a daily time
alone with God any easier.

My father once told me something that discouraged
me. But then the more I thought about it, the more it
encouraged me. He was a Christian from his boyhood.
As a youth he began studying the Bible and having his
personal quiet time every day, early in the morning. As a
small boy I used to like to get up early (something that
wore off fast as I got older!). But I never seemed able
to get up ahead of my father. I would go downstairs and
see my father there at 5:30 in the morning every day, on his
knees, with an open Bible and a prayer list in front of him.
It was an unalterable pattern with him and had been
for forty years.

Yet he said to me towards the end of his life, "Dave, it is
no easier today to get up early and have my quiet time than
it was forty years ago."

And I thought, "Oh, no! Of all the discouraging things!"

But then I began to realize that he was a living example
that it could be done. He did it day in and day out, week in
and week out, year after year for forty years. So it can be
done.

He was a man who also lived a busy life. He was involved
in many activities and he always had plenty to do. But he
never allowed anything to interfere with his day-by-day
meeting alone with God. So he did not become like a
shrub in the desert or an uninhabited salt land, because he

88

knew how to get that daily renewal and refreshment from God.

On the wall of my office hangs a poster that speaks to me often. In the days prior to the Urbana Convention, when I would be overwhelmed with the amount of work to do, I would look and read that poster. It is a prayer that I need to be praying constantly. It goes like this:

> Slow me down, Lord.
>
> Ease the pounding of my heart by the
> quieting of my mind.
>
> Steady my hurried pace with a vision of
> the eternal reach of time.
>
> Give me, amid the confusion of the day,
> the calmness of the everlasting hills.
>
> Break the tensions of my nerves and
> muscles with the soothing music of the
> singing streams that live in my memory.
> Help me to know the magical, restoring
> power of sleep.
>
> Teach me the art of taking minute
> vacations—of slowing down to look at a
> flower, to chat with a friend, to pat a dog, to
> read a few lines from a good book.
>
> Slow me down, Lord, and inspire me to
> send my roots deep into the soil of life's
> enduring values that I may grow
> toward the stars of my greater destiny.

I need that prayer constantly, that God would slow me down, that I do not become like a barren, parched, uninhabited salt land.

89

CHAPTER EIGHT

"Blessed Is the Man Who Trusts in the Lord"

The Place of the Word of God

Jeremiah has talked about a curse for the man who trusts in man. But now there is a promise of blessing.

> "Blessed is the man who trusts in the Lord,
> whose trust is the Lord. He is like a tree planted by
> water, that sends out its roots by the stream, and does
> not fear when heat comes, for its leaves remain
> green, and is not anxious in the year of drought,
> for it does not cease to bear fruit." (Jeremiah 17:7,
> 8)

In this case, I like the way the King James Version words the second part of this verse—"whose hope the Lord is." What does it mean to trust in the Lord?

Jeremiah illustrates this repeatedly throughout the book. First, it is belief in God Himself, belief that God is the One Who is at work.

91

THE HOPE OF JEREMIAH

O Lord, thou knowest; remember me and visit me,
and take vengeance for me on my persecutors....
(Jeremiah 15:15)

Notice that first phrase, "O Lord, thou knowest..."
An expanded paraphrase could be, "Lord, you know all
about what I am going through. You know these problems.
You know the despair. You know the temptation, Lord.
You know all about it."

Amy Carmichael was a great missionary who lived for
fifty years in India without ever returning to England. She
lived in a sickroom for many of those years because of an
accident suffered early in her missionary career. I am
told that she had two plaques on the wall of her room. One
said, "Fear not." The other said, "I know."

"O Lord, thou knowest." Jeremiah could turn to the
Lord and say, "Lord, you know what I am going
through." So Jeremiah was learning to trust in the Lord by
saying, "O Lord, since you know all about this, I am leaving it
in your hands entirely."

One of the things that used to rebuke me about the
humble believers we knew in Colombia was the simplicity
of their faith. They gladly accepted the fact that God knew all
about what they were going through. They were willing to
leave things in God's hands.

One year I was traveling through the backwoods area at
Eastertime, and came to the little village of Macedonia. (That
wasn't the original name of the village. But when almost all
the village had become Christians, they had given
themselves a biblical name. They often did that when a
whole village would come to the Lord.) The people in
Macedonia told me an interesting story.

In that same area of the forest was another village

92

which was a Communist training center. I had also been through that village. It was entirely inhabited by Communists who were in a training program to infiltrate the jungles, work with the peasants, and take over political power in that area. One of the Communists from that village had come to Macedonia during Easter week. Pulling a box of matches out of his pocket, he said to one of the Christians, "Do you see this box of matches?"

The Christian said, "Yes."

"I am going to burn down your chapel on Good Friday with these matches."

The chapel was built of thatched roof and bamboo, so it would burn readily.

The Christian said, "That's interesting, but that is not up to you."

The Communist said, "Oh, it isn't? Who is it up to?"

"Well, it is up to God."

"Oh, is that so?" said the Communist who, of course, was an atheist. "We'll see about that."

The Christian said, "Yes, we will see about that."

When I arrived two days after Easter, the chapel was still standing. I said, "What happened?"

"Oh," they said, "he was bitten by a snake on Thursday and he died."

It didn't really bother them when he had threatened to burn down their chapel. They believed that God knew all about it, that they were in God's hands, and that God would, one way or another, work out His plan. His plan in that case was to remove that man before he had a chance to burn down the chapel. The point was that these people were simply trusting God. They said, "You know all about it, Lord." Jeremiah says, "O Lord, thou knowest." His belief was in God Himself.

Second, his belief was in God's Word.

> Thy words were found, and I ate them, and thy
> words became to me a joy and the delight of my
> heart; for I am called by thy name, O Lord, God of
> hosts. (Jeremiah 15:16)

The Word of God became wonderfully living and real to
him. The Word of God can become to us the daily
delight that we so desperately need. Once again, this is
something that we know in our heads, but has it really gotten
into our hearts? Is the Word of God daily meeting your
need? Has it met your need today? Are you finding in
the Word of God that joy and courage that you need day
by day?

Following Urbana 73, Inter-Varsity wanted to know
what my future plans were. I had been on loan from the
Latin America Mission to Inter-Varsity for a period of six
years. Dr. John Alexander, president of Inter-Varsity,
wanted to name the director of Urbana 76 fairly soon so
that work on the next convention could get started. He
asked me to accept that responsibility. So I had to let him
know if I was going to continue with Inter-Varsity or if God
was leading us back to Latin America.

My personal desire was very strong to return to Latin
America. I told my wife repeatedly during the months that
we were praying about this, "If I were to make up my mind
on the basis of what I personally want to do, we would go
back to Colombia tomorrow without question." This
was not because I did not enjoy Inter-Varsity work. I love
being with students. But my heart is so deeply rooted in
Colombia that I would give anything to return. I love the
Colombian people with all my heart and would rather
be there than anywhere else on the face of the earth. We

prayed and struggled about this for several months without coming to any conclusion.

Finally, I decided to set aside a day for prayer and fasting when I would study the Word, pray, and seek God's will. On that day I would ask God to reveal His will for me. I had no idea how God would lead or what methods He would use to show me His will. Then the Lord did a wonderful thing through the Scriptures.

The day that I had set aside as a day of prayer was a Monday. On Sunday night at church our pastor preached on the story of the birth of Moses. It was a good message. I enjoyed it but I didn't see any particular application to my own need at that time.

The next morning in my quiet time, my regular reading brought me to the story of the birth of Moses. Again I enjoyed it, although I still didn't see any immediate application for me.

Later that morning I called up one of my great prayer partners. She is an elderly Chinese lady named Christiana Tsai, and she lives near Lancaster, Pennsylvania. She is a converted Buddhist who has been in a darkened room for forty-three years. She has a rare disease which has affected her entire body, including her eyesight. She cannot look at the light and must be in a darkened room all the time. You can go into her room and sense immediately that the power of the Holy Spirit is there. Because she can't sleep well, living in constant pain, she spends long hours in prayer day and night.

I called Miss Tsai that morning to tell her that this was the day I was seeking God's will. She did two things.

First, she burst out over the telephone with a word of wisdom from God. She occasionally has the ability to speak and one feels as though it is God speaking His wisdom

95

through her. She said, "Dave Howard, you stay with
Inter-Varsity. This is God's will for you. I have
absolutely no doubt about it." She went on for about five
minutes explaining why I should stay with Inter-Varsity.

Then she began to talk about the birth of Moses,
drawing some lessons out of this and applying them to
me. She talked for another ten minutes, giving me some
scriptural exhortations.

I hung up the phone, opened my Bible, and read the first
three chapters of Exodus again. Then I prayed, "Lord,
what are You trying to say to me from the story of the
birth of Moses? That's three times in about twelve hours
that this passage has come directly to me from Your Word."

Now I don't hear voices and I didn't hear a voice then,
but it was one of those cases where it came clearly to
mind what God was trying to say. It was this: The greatest
crisis in the life of Moses took place at the burning bush
when God asked Moses to do something that he didn't
want to do. What was it that He asked him to do? He
wanted Moses to go and work with his own people.

The Lord said to me, "Dave, I know that you want to go
back to Colombia, but I want you to stay and work with
your own people. I know you would rather work with
Colombians. I know that is where your heart is. But just as
I asked Moses to do something that he did not want to do, I
am asking you to do this and stay here."

By noontime that day, as I had continued to pray,
there was no doubt in my mind that this was the Word of
God for me. So I came to the conclusion that this was
God's plan. The Word of God became to me the joy and
rejoicing of my heart. It became just what I needed as the
Lord met my need through the Word.

Notice one more thing about the man who trusts in

God. Jeremiah trusted in the Lord Himself. He trusted in the Word. Then he acted on the Word.

> If I say, "I will not mention him, or speak any more in his name," there is in my heart as it were a burning fire shut up in my bones, and I am weary with holding it in, and I cannot. (Jeremiah 20:9)

Fire in my bones! The Word of God became so impelling to him that he had to act on it. "Blessed is the man who trusts in the Lord." As he learns to trust in the Lord and in the Word of the Lord, God's Word becomes in him a burning fire and he *must* speak it out. As you and I become saturated more and more in the Word of God, the Word will become to us a burning fire which must be permitted to come out.

What are the results of this for the man who is trusting in the Lord?

> He is like a tree planted by water, that sends out its roots by the stream, and does not fear when heat comes, for its leaves remain green, and is not anxious in the year of drought, for it does not cease to bear fruit. (Jeremiah 17:8)

The concept is identical to that expressed in Psalm 1.

> Blessed is the man who walks not in the counsel of the wicked, nor stands in the way of sinners, nor sits in the seat of scoffers; but his delight is in the law of the Lord, and on his law he meditates day and night. He is like a tree planted by streams of water, that yields its fruit in its season, and its leaf does not wither. In all that he does, he prospers. (Psalm 1:1-3)

97

Jeremiah is saying the same thing. The man who trusts in the Lord is putting his roots down deep and sucking up the water. Then he doesn't have to fear when heat comes, because his leaves remain green. He is not anxious in the year of drought, for he does not cease to bear fruit. If you and I are learning to get our roots down deep into the Word of God day by day, that water is coming up into our lifeblood and flowing out. And when the heat comes (and it will come) we will not wither, because the life of God is there, coming from those deep roots.

Jeremiah has an amazing example of this in his own life. It is one of the most startling parts of the book. It is a perfect illustration of a man who has his roots down deep. And when the heat comes, he continues to give forth fruit.

> The word that came to Jeremiah from the Lord in the tenth year of Zedekiah king of Judah, which was the eighteenth year of Nebuchadrezzar. At that time the army of the king of Babylon was besieging Jerusalem, and Jeremiah the prophet was shut up in the court of the guard which was in the palace of the king of Judah. (Jeremiah 32:1, 2)

Now this was at the very end of the kingdom of Judah. Zedekiah was the last king of Judah. Jeremiah had been prophesying since the thirteenth year of Josiah. He had continued right through the reign of five different kings. Now Zedekiah is in his final days. He reigned for eleven years, and this is in the tenth year. Nebuchadnezzar (or Nebuchadrezzar) is besieging Jerusalem. The city is going to fall. The walls will be destroyed. The Temple will be burnt with fire. Judah will be carried off into Babylon for seventy years. Jeremiah has already foretold all of this. He knows the end is near. But right in the middle of this, he makes an incredible decision. Jeremiah said:

> "The word of the Lord came to me: Behold,
> Hanamel the son of Shallum your uncle will
> come to you and say, 'Buy my field which is at
> Anathoth, for the right of redemption by purchase is
> yours.' Then Hanamel my cousin came to me in
> the court of the guard, in accordance with the
> word of the Lord, and said to me, 'Buy my field
> which is at Anathoth in the land of Benjamin, for the
> right of possession and redemption is yours; buy it
> for yourself.' Then I knew that this was the word
> of the Lord." (Jeremiah 32:6-8)

Now who in his right mind would buy a field when the
kingdom is disintegrating, the city is besieged, and there is
no hope of deliverance? Jeremiah knew it better than
anyone else. This is the end of the long siege. Then
suddenly Jeremiah's cousin comes along with the wild idea
that he buy some real estate! Who could be foolish enough
to do a ridiculous thing like that? Yet Jeremiah says:

> "And I bought the field at Anathoth from
> Hanamel my cousin, and weighed out the money to
> him, seventeen shekels of silver. I signed the deed,
> sealed it, got witnesses, and weighed the money
> on scales. Then I took the sealed deed of purchase,
> containing the terms and conditions, and the open
> copy; and I gave the deed of purchase to Baruch
> the son of Neriah son of Mahseiah, in the
> presence of Hanamel my cousin, in the presence of
> the witnesses who signed the deed of purchase, and
> in the presence of all the Jews who were sitting in
> the court of the guard. I charged Baruch in their

presence, saying, 'Thus says the Lord of hosts, the
God of Israel: Take these deeds, both this sealed
deed of purchase and this open deed, and put them
in an earthenware vessel, that they may last for a
long time. For thus says the Lord of hosts, the God
of Israel: Houses and fields and vineyards shall again
be bought in this land.' " (Jeremiah 31.9-15)

Do you see what has happened to Jeremiah? The heat
is on now. Nebuchadnezzar has surrounded the city. The
walls are beginning to crumble. The city is about to fall.
Judah is about to be carried off into captivity. Yet
Jeremiah buys a field! What confidence and trust in
God! He must have said to himself, "Someday we are
coming back, and I want my family to own that field. I will
leave it here in my name. I will sign the deed, seal it, have
witnesses, take it up to the scribe, and put it away in an
earthen vessel for safety." He does not wither when the
heat comes. He knows that God is going to do what God said
he would do. Remember what God said to him in his call:
"I am watching over my word to perform it" (Jeremiah
1:12).

"So, Jeremiah, don't wither in the heat. Keep those roots
down deep, and the water of life flows out."

So when you and I find ourselves under great
pressure, the results can be great fruitfulness if our roots
are deep enough in the Word of God.

CHAPTER NINE

"The Heart Is Deceitful above All Things"

A *Warning for the Servant of God*

We come now to a grave warning:

> The heart is deceitful above all things, and
> desperately corrupt; who can understand it? "I
> the Lord search the mind and try the heart, to give
> to every man according to his ways, according to the
> fruit of his doings." (Jeremiah 17:9, 10)

What is the connection between the previous
passages (discussed in the last chapter) and this one? There
is a great danger of confusing fleshly action and trust in the
Lord. Jeremiah has just said, "Cursed is the man who trusts
in man ... Blessed is the man who trusts in the Lord." It
is very easy, at times, to confuse those two things—to
think that we are trusting in the Lord when really we are
carrying out fleshly activity. It is so easy to deceive
ourselves by thinking that activity is spirituality. I think

101

I am trusting in the Lord when I am actually trusting in myself or my service.

We have a beautiful illustration of that in the New Testament story of the two sisters, Mary and Martha. When Jesus came to their house, Martha was busy preparing the dinner. She became upset because Mary was not helping in the kitchen. Mary was sitting at Jesus' feet.

Remember Jesus' word to Martha? "Martha, Martha, you are anxious and troubled about many things. One thing is needful. Mary has chosen the good portion which shall not be taken away from her" (Luke 10:41, 42). Jesus was saying that even more important than activity is that you should sit at His feet and learn from Him.

We often tend to fault Martha at this point and say, "Well, Martha was all in the wrong." Do you recall the rest of the story of Martha? She appears again in the Scriptures. The last time she appears, do you know what she is doing? Exactly the same thing! But she is doing it now with the right motive. She is again putting on a dinner for Jesus. It is after Lazarus was raised from the dead. Jesus comes to their home and once again Martha is serving. Jesus doesn't rebuke her this time. Why? Because now she has learned to balance her activity with that "good portion" of learning from the Lord.

Martha had certain gifts. Jesus wasn't saying, "Don't use those gifts, don't ever go into the kitchen again." What Jesus said was, "Martha, put things into perspective. Get them in the right balance. Mary knows where to start. Now, Martha, you get them into balance." And Martha did.

The next time Jesus comes to their home, Martha does the same thing, but she does it with a calm and beautiful spirit. Jesus has no rebuke for her now; she has learned to put together faith and works. She has learned to sit at Jesus' feet as Mary did. And Jesus is telling her now, "Let's get these things together. Don't trust in the flesh. Trust in the Lord." But the heart is deceitful above all things, and desperately corrupt, so it is easy to confuse these things. Satan is so subtle that he will get in through our deceitful hearts and make us think that fleshly activity is really trusting in the Lord.

That is why this paragraph in Jeremiah comes right after his comments about the cursing of the man who trusts in the flesh and the blessing of the man who trusts in the Lord. Jeremiah warns, "But be careful. The heart is deceitful above all things, and desperately corrupt...." Recognize how easy it is to confuse those two things and to think you are trusting in the Lord when really you are trusting in men!

If you know your heart, as I know my heart, you know the awful corruption that exists there. Seneca, the Roman philosopher, said, "Every man knows that about his own heart which he would not dare tell to his closest friend."

Alexander Whyte was deeply conscious of the sinfulness of the human heart. Preaching on "Paul as the chief of sinners," he quoted several great divines who were overwhelmed by their own corruption.

> "Do not mistake me," said Jacob Behman, "for my heart is as full as it can hold of all malice at you and all ill-will. My heart is the very dunghill of the Devil, and it is no easy work to wrestle with him on his own chosen ground. But wrestle with him on that ground of his I must, and that the whole of my life to the end."
>
> "Begone! all ye self-ignorant and false flatterers," shouted Philip Neve at them; "I am

103

good for nothing but to do evil."

"When a man like me," says Luther, "comes to know the plague of his own heart, he is not miserable only—he is absolute misery itself; he is not sinful only—he is absolute sin itself."

"I am made of sin," sobbed Bishop Andrews, till his private prayer book was all but unreadable to his heirs because of its author's sweat and tears.

"It has often appeared to me," says Jonathan Edwards, "that if God were to mark my heart-iniquity my bed would be in hell."

"I sat down on the side of a stank," says Lord Brodie, "and was disgusted at the toads and many other unclean creatures I saw sweltering there. But all the time my own heart was far worse earth to me, and filthier by far than the filthy earth I sat upon."[1]

Then Whyte summarized this sense of sin by saying,

"The holiest of men are the most full of holy fear, holy penitence, holy humility, and holy love. And all that is so because the more true spirituality of mind any man has, the more exquisite will be that man's sensibility to sin and to the exceeding sinfulness of sin."[2]

Living for Christ puts you into a spiritual battle. When you step out in God's service, you voluntarily put yourself in a vulnerable position, right on the front lines. In time of battle, it is those fighting on the front that get hurt. The commanding officer knows that some are going to fall.

---

[1]Whyte, *op. cit.,* Vol. II, p. 247, 248.
[2]*Ibid,* p. 249.

"The Heart Is Deceitful above All Things"

You gave yourself to God and offered voluntarily to move
out into His service. Satan doesn't want you there. You
are in the line of fire. Your heart is desperately wicked,
as my heart is desperately wicked. We dare not think that
we will be immune from those things that could destroy our
effectiveness in God's army. There is nothing that Satan
would rather do than get us out of the battle line. One
of the best ways he can do this involves our desperately
corrupt heart. The lust of the flesh, the lust of the eye, and
the pride of life could so overwhelm us as to make us
useless in the work of God. Nothing would please Satan
more. It is a sobering thought to realize that no matter
how old a person is, he never gets out of the line of fire if he
is serving the Lord.

Years ago in Colombia we had experienced some real
problems in the churches. Then one year there seemed to
be a great awakening, with a rising of strong national
leadership. At the beginning of the year, at the annual
church convention, the finest Administrative
Committee any of us could remember was elected to
direct the church work for the coming year. They were
strong men. One was the spiritual father of most of the
other pastors and had been God's instrument in opening
up that whole area to the gospel many years before. He
had been in the ministry almost thirty years. Most of the
other men on the Committee were spiritual children of
his.

In July of that year, I received a letter from the church
which the president of the Administrative Committee was
pastoring. They asked me to come and help them work out
a problem. The pastor was being accused of adultery. I
went down to that city sick at heart. I went, not because I
had any authority but simply because they were asking me, as

105

a brother in Christ, to come and help them deal with this issue.

Upon arriving in the city, I went to the elders of the church to find out what the accusations were. I took with me a pastor from another church, because I felt that in a case like this there had to be at least two witnesses involved.

We went finally to the pastor himself who was being accused. I laid out the accusations, asking his reactions to them. It was one of the saddest days of my life. Here was this great man of God who for nearly thirty years had been wonderfully used in leading many others to Christ and had taught younger men and led them into the pastorate. He did not deny the accusations. I turned away that afternoon absolutely sick at heart.

He went to the church that night and asked forgiveness. The church decided to give him a second chance.

Three months later I was in Costa Rica on some mission business when I received a letter from a colleague, informing me that the same pastor had been accused again of indiscreet actions. To our deep sorrow, the accusations again proved true, and he had to be removed from the ministry.

About the same time, I got a call from another city where the treasurer of the Administrative Committee was the pastor of the local church. They said, "Would you please come to our church? We have good evidence that the pastor is embezzling funds." As treasurer of the Administrative Committee, he had money in his hands. The temptation was there.

I went to that church and sat down with the pastor. I spent a whole day with him, trying to find out the truth of the matter. It appeared that the accusations were true, but I could not get him to recognize it. The result, when the evidence became conclusive, was that he had to be removed from the ministry.

A couple of months later, I was again in Costa Rica on mission business when I got another letter from my colleague saying, "Dave, Pedro has come to us and admitted fornication." He was the secretary of the Administrative Committee. The four officers of that Committee were considered the finest group in many years. Yet now the president had fallen into adultery, the treasurer was out because of dishonest use of funds, and now the secretary had confessed to fornication.

When the vice-president heard this, he resigned in protest against the others. Thus the entire slate of outstanding officers was gone. Our hearts wept as we saw this happening. The truth of Galatians 6:1 came home strongly:

> Brethren, if a man is overtaken in any trespass, you who are spiritual should restore him in a spirit of gentleness. Look to yourself, lest you too be tempted.

It was sobering and heartrending to see these leaders fall. It was especially sad to see the oldest pastor who had walked with the Lord much longer than I and had been out in the battle, yet was finally caught by the arrows of Satan. And I realized the desperate corruptness of my own heart and how easy it would be for Satan to get to me too. Age didn't make any difference. Serving the Lord for thirty years makes a man no more immune than anyone else to those attacks.

If you are out on the front lines, you can expect attacks of the enemy. They might not come in those same areas. But you can be certain that Satan is after you. You know the

weakness of your own heart. Jeremiah's words are true:
"The heart is deceitful above all things, and desperately
corrupt; who can understand it? 'I the Lord search the mind
and try the heart, to give to every man according to his
ways, according to the fruit of his doings.' "

A phrase from 2 Samuel 1:19b describes how we felt at
that time in Colombia: "How are the mighty fallen!" How
those mighty men of God fell under the attack of Satan!
We need to use the whole armor of God to be able to
stand against the wiles of the devil.

CHAPTER TEN

"A Glorious Throne Set on High"

The Sanctuary for the Servant of God

Finally, Jeremiah gives us a solution to all of this. He has talked about a curse. He has talked about a blessing. He has given a grave warning. Then he turns and provides a great remedy for the servant in danger.

> A glorious throne set on high from the beginning is the place of our sanctuary. (Jeremiah 17:12)

Before the glorious throne of God, we find our sanctuary. How does he describe that throne? It is a glorious throne, it is set on high, and it is from the beginning. That is, it is an eternal throne. Jeremiah is saying, "That great glorious throne of God is the place of my sanctuary. That is where I must go to find my protection. It is there that I see the glory of God. It is there that I see God set on high, ruling over all. It is there that I see that God is from the beginning, and He is the one who said to me when He first called me, 'I am watching over my

109

word to perform it.' He sits on that glorious high throne, set on high from the beginning." Jeremiah sees the glory of God.

The Psalmist exhorted Israel to "declare his glory among the nations..." (Psalm 96:3a). He wanted to see God's glory declared throughout the world. Jeremiah says, "It is a glorious throne where I find my place of sanctuary. It provides for me a place of protection in the midst of all this pressure, when the heat of battle comes and temptations attack me." Jeremiah knew more about that than most other prophets and Christians who ever lived.

This is similar to what the Psalmist described:

> But as for me, my feet had almost stumbled, my steps had well nigh slipped. For I was envious of the arrogant, when I saw the prosperity of the wicked. For they have no pangs; their bodies are sound and sleek. They are not in trouble as other men are; they are not stricken like other men. Therefore pride is their necklace; violence covers them as a garment. (Psalm 73:2-6)

Finally, having described the apparent prosperity of the wicked, the Psalmist says in desperation:

> But when I thought how to understand this, it seemed to me a wearisome task, until I went into the sanctuary of God; then I perceived their end. (Psalm 73:16, 17)

That is when I came to grips with the whole thing—when I went into the sanctuary of God. *Then* I perceived their end! Then I saw that it is God who is watching over His Word to perform it. Then in that sanctuary, where I saw the glorious throne set on high, I knew that the Lord of the universe, the Creator of all mankind, was still holding everything in His hand.

Jeremiah says in the midst of all of this—the cursing, the blessing, the warning—there is a glorious throne set on high and I must turn to that throne. It is the only place to which I can turn.

> O Lord, the hope of Israel, all who forsake thee shall be put to shame.... (Jeremiah 17:13)

He declares that God is the hope of Israel. Jeremiah is a discouraging book, but there are many places where he speaks of hope. Look, for example, at Chapter 29 where he comes with a great outburst of hope. He knows what is going to happen.

> "For thus says the Lord: When seventy years are completed for Babylon, I will visit you, and I will fulfil to you my promise and bring you back to this place. For I know the plans I have for you, says the Lord, plans for welfare and not for evil, to give you a future and a hope. Then you will call upon me and come and pray to me, and I will hear you. You will seek me and find me; when you seek me with all your heart, I will be found by you, says the Lord, and I will restore your fortunes and gather you from all the nations and all the places where I have driven you, says the Lord, and I will bring you back to the place from which I sent you into exile." (Jeremiah 29:10-14)

God says, "I know. I know all about it, and I am going to bring you back." This is discovered in the place of His sanctuary. He invites us into His sanctuary for the rest and renewal we need.

111

THE HOPE OF JEREMIAH

Come ye yourselves apart and rest awhile,
  Weary, I know it, of the press and throng,
Wipe from your brow the sweat and dust of toil,
  And in my quiet strength again be strong.

Come ye aside from all the world holds dear,
  For converse which the world has never known,
Alone with me and with My Father here,
  With me and with My Father not alone.

Come, tell me all that you have said and done,
  Your victories and failures, hopes and fears,
I know how hardly souls are wooed and won;
  My choicest wreaths are always wet with tears.

Come ye and rest: the journey is too great,
  And you will faint beside the way and sink:
The bread of life is here for you to eat,
  And here for you the wine of love to drink.

Then, fresh from converse with your Lord, return
  And work till daylight softens into even:
The brief hours are not lost in which ye learn
  More of your Master and His rest in heaven.
                    —Edward Henry Bickersteth

In the place of His sanctuary He waits for us to come and
worship the glorious One sitting on that high throne. Then
we will have the hope, the courage, and the strength to
face the dangers and discouragements that surround us.

PART FOUR

Christ and Jeremiah

*Now when Jesus came into the district of
Caesarea Philippi, he asked his disciples,
"Who do men say that the Son of Man is?"
And they said, "Some say John the Baptist,
others say Elijah, and others Jeremiah or one of
the prophets."*

Matthew 16:13, 14

*Remember my affliction and my bitterness, the
wormwood and the gall! My soul continually
thinks of it and is bowed down within me.
But this I call to mind, and therefore I have
hope: The steadfast love of the Lord never ceases,
his mercies never come to an end; they are new
every morning; great is thy faithfulness.
"The Lord is my portion," says my soul,
"therefore I will hope in him."*

Lamentations 3:19-24

CHAPTER ELEVEN

"A Man of Sorrows and Acquainted with Grief"

The Personality of Jeremiah

There are nine references to Jeremiah in the Bible outside of his book. Six of those are in the Old Testament, three in the New, in the Gospel of Matthew. Two of the Matthew references simply quote him. The third is very intriguing.

> Now when Jesus came into the district of Caesarea Philippi, he asked his disciples, "Who do men say that the Son of Man is?" And they said, "Some say John the Baptist, others say Elijah, and others Jeremiah or one of the prophets." (Matthew 16:13, 14)

Now I can understand why they would confuse Jesus with John the Baptist. Jesus was preaching repentance. He had scathing rebukes for the hypocrites within the organized religion of the day. He had a lot of the same things to say that John the Baptist had been saying. It would be easy to confuse the two.

I can understand why they would confuse Him with Elijah. Jesus was performing many of the same kinds of miracles. He raised people from the dead. He provided food for the hungry. Much of what Jesus was doing was similar to the things that Elijah had done.

But why would anyone confuse Jesus with Jeremiah? Why, of all the prophets of the Old Testament, did they say, "This is Jeremiah come back again"? One writer put it this way:

> The most exquisite sensibility of soul was
> Jeremiah's singular and sovereign distinction
> above all the other Hebrew prophets. Such another
> child for sensibility of soul was not born of woman
> until the Virgin Mary brought forth the Man of
> Sorrows Himself.[1]

Why did people confuse Christ with Jeremiah? There must have been something about their understanding of Jeremiah which made them say, when Jesus of Nazareth came along, "This could be Jeremiah come back to life again."

What kind of personality did Jeremiah have? We have already seen something of it as we watched him react to his call and ministry. The descriptions of Jesus Christ as "a man of sorrows and acquainted with grief" would fit well with Jeremiah. We remember Jeremiah as the "weeping prophet," the one who said, "O that my eyes were a flood of tears" and the man who repeatedly poured out his soul for his people. He was a man who knew how to weep. Jesus also knew how to weep. Twice in the Scriptures we

[1]Whyte, *op. cit.,* Vol. I, p. 395.

are told specifically that Jesus wept. I am sure that He must have wept on other occasions too. But these two occasions are described for us.

We see Him weeping over Jerusalem in Luke 19:41: "And when he drew near and saw the city he wept over it." He pours out His heart and weeps over this city that has put to death the prophets and that will soon be destroyed again.

He weeps again at the tomb of Lazarus in John 11. Why did He weep at the tomb of Lazarus? No doubt part of the reason was that He felt deeply for Mary and Martha who were suffering over the loss of their brother. It is interesting to notice that when Jesus first heard about the death of Lazarus, He did not weep. It wasn't until He arrived at the tomb that He wept. Now why was that? In Alexander Whyte's character study on Lazarus, he has a fascinating angle as to why Jesus wept at the tomb of Lazarus. It may help us understand Jeremiah as well.

Alexander Whyte had a sanctified imagination. He would try to put himself into the shoes of the men and women of the Bible about whom he was writing or preaching. As he did so, he would come up with unique ideas that most of us never would have thought of. He quotes Chrysologus, commenting on the tomb of Lazarus.

> "When our Lord was told of Lazarus' death He was glad. But when He came to raise him to life, He wept. For, though His disciples gained by it, and though Martha and Mary gained by it, yet Lazarus himself lost by it, by being re-imprisoned, re-committed, and re-submitted to the manifold incommodities of this life."[2]

[2]Whyte, *op. cit.,* Vol. II, p. 56.

CHRIST AND JEREMIAH

Jesus was weeping, says Chrysologus, because He had to call Lazarus back to the imprisonments of this life. Talk about culture shock! Imagine coming back to the earth from where he had been! Jesus knew He had to bring him back and so He wept. Then Whyte imagines the scene in heaven:

> And thus it was that scarcely had Lazarus sat down in his Father's house, he had not got his harp of gold well into his hand, he had not got the hallelujah that they were preparing against the Ascension of their Lord well into his mouth, when the angel Gabriel came up to where he sat, all rapture through and through, and said to him: "Hail! Lazarus: highly honored among the glorified from among men. Thy Master calls up for thee. He has some service for thee still to do for Him on the earth." And the sound of many waters fell silent for a season as they saw one of the most shining of their number rise up, and lay aside his glory, hang his harp on the wall, and pass out of their sight, and descend to where their heavenly Prince still tarried with His work unfinished.[3]

What a picture! Here is Lazarus called by God back into that vale of sorrow and tears, back into the imprisonments of human flesh, for the glory of God. Jesus wept when He saw this because He knew what was coming for Lazarus.

There must have been something of this in the heart of Jeremiah as he wept over his people. He saw what was coming, and he wept because he knew what his people were going to have to endure. God had allowed him to

[3]Ibid.

see the future, and Jeremiah wept. So he was a man of sorrows and acquainted with grief.

He was also "despised and rejected of men." We have seen how he was cast into prison many times, how he was beaten, how he was thrown into the cistern, how his word was rejected, how the king cut up the scroll with the Word of God on it and burned it up. He had that constant rejection that also became familiar to the Son of Man.

Such rejection must have thrown Jeremiah more completely than ever on the Lord. It must have etched into his life a depth of character and a spiritual relationship with God which was similar to what Jesus Christ had. When Christ was despised and rejected of men, He held on to His faith in His father. Although He was the Son of God, He was also the Son of Man. He understood suffering from the human viewpoint. Through suffering He had built into Him that character and strength which comes with constant opposition.

It is not easy to be despised and rejected of other men, but it will throw us into greater confidence in God.

In July 1974 I was privileged to attend the International Congress on World Evangelization in Lausanne, Switzerland. They asked me to lead a workshop entitled, "Witnessing under Hostile Governments." I wasn't quite sure why they asked me except that I had lived in Colombia during a period of great opposition. I almost turned it down because I felt unqualified. However, I finally accepted and was glad that I did because of the people who came to that workshop.

At Lausanne, over 150 different nations were represented. Those who came to my workshop were mostly from countries where they live under government opposition. They came to discuss what it means to be a

119

Christian and to witness for Jesus Christ in lands where this is against the law. There were men and women from Hungary, Yugoslavia, Poland, Rumania, Russia, Nepal, Afghanistan. To hear those Christians discuss together what it means to be despised and rejected of men was sobering. Dr. J. Christy Wilson, who had lived for twenty years in Afghanistan, wrote the study paper for the workshop. He presented an excellent biblical foundation for witnessing under opposition.

There were three pastors from Hungary. They were very cautious about what they would say. They were convinced, I think, that the Congress was infiltrated with spies from their country and that anything they said could later be held against them. They were frightened when they learned that we recorded these workshops. When we discovered this, we stopped recording and destroyed the tape of the first day. They seemed to relax more after that. One believer from Rumania was also very guarded about what he would say. We tried to draw out a young man from Poland, but he didn't feel too free to talk much either. He knew only too well what it was to be despised and rejected of men in his own country, and he didn't want to get caught unnecessarily.

Two Russians came to the workshop. Just to see their faces was an experience in itself. Their faces reflected the character that had been built into them by having been despised and rejected of men most of their lives. We asked them, "Which church do you belong to in Russia? Do you belong to the registered church, which is recognized by the government and so can meet publicly, or are you from the underground church?"

They said, "We are from the underground church."

We asked them to describe the difference. They told us

that in order to be registered, they have to promise that they will not teach religion to their children, they will not propagate their religion outside the church, they will not distribute Bibles, they will not have young peoples' training programs. If they will agree to that, then they can worship together unmolested.

One of these men said, "Every Christian in Russia has to decide for himself which way he will go. For my part, I could not go that pathway. I chose to go underground and spend my life fleeing from the police."

And that is what he has done. He has been caught and has served time in the slave labor camps of northern Siberia about which Alexander Solzhenitsyn has written so brilliantly. He had been used of God to start an underground church in the slave labor camp, which is still going on. To hear those men share what it means to be despised and rejected of men, and to see the character in their faces and the joy with which they talked about it, was unforgettable.

There was one Christian there from Nepal, the only Christian that was able to come from that Himalayan country. He sat quietly for the first two days in our workshop. We didn't want to embarrass him, yet if he had anything to share we wanted to hear it. So on the third day of the workshop I turned to him and said, "Brother, if you feel that you could share with us what it costs in your land to be a Christian, we would love to hear from you."

"Yes," he said, "I'll be glad to speak. Let me tell you what it means to be a Christian in Nepal. We say in our country that the birth certificate of a Christian is one year in jail. The baptismal certificate of a Christian is six years in jail. The minute you are baptized publicly, you can assume that the next six years will be spent in jail. This is the way it is in our land. If you are a Christian, you have a birth certificate and a baptismal certificate, and they add up to seven years in jail."

These men have been despised and rejected of men. They have been oppressed and afflicted. But the character that has been forged in their lives is reminiscent of the prophet Jeremiah.

I wish you could have heard one prayer meeting that we had in our workshop. At the end of one session, we had gotten so much information from these men and women about suffering in their lands that we were moved to pray. I suggested that we spend the last fifteen minutes of the workshop in prayer. I don't know how many languages were used in prayer that day. I didn't understand most of them, of course, but there was a great outpouring of prayer.

The minute I said that we were going to pray, everyone bowed their head. But the two Russians stood up stiff as ramrods. There was a Finnish man there who spoke English and Russian. He turned to me and said, "Our Russian brothers are accustomed to standing when they pray." So I told the rest of the group and everyone else stood. When they come to the presence of the Lord, out of pure respect, they stand. So the whole group stood and prayed together for fifteen minutes in many different languages.

The two Russians were the first to pray. Even though most of us couldn't understand them, there was a sense of unity in praying with them. There was a great outpouring of worship and supplication to God. It was one of the most moving times in prayer that I have ever experienced.

These people have been despised and rejected,

oppressed and afflicted. They were men of sorrows. They could tell us stories that drew forth tears because of the suffering they had been through. That is one reason why Jesus Christ was confused with Jeremiah. He was despised and rejected, a man of sorrows and acquainted with grief. And so was Jeremiah. So when Jesus of Nazareth came along they said, "This man is just like Jeremiah."

CHAPTER TWELVE

"Grace in the Wilderness"

The Message of Jeremiah

What about the message of Jeremiah? Let's consider first what the Scriptures say about the teaching of Christ. This may help us to understand better the message of Jeremiah and why the message of Christ could have been confused with it.

The Gospel of Luke tells us:

> And they were all amazed and said to one another, "What is this word? For with authority and power he commands the unclean spirits, and they come out." (Luke 4:36)

This man preaches with authority and power. He commands the unclean spirits and they come out. They said, "That is the way Jeremiah was. He preached with *authority*."

Jeremiah said:

"They have spoken falsely of the Lord, and have
said, 'He will do nothing; no evil will come upon us,
nor shall we see sword or famine. The prophets
will become wind; the word is not in them. Thus
shall it be done to them!' " Therefore thus says the
Lord, the God of hosts: "Because they have spoken
this word, behold, I am making my words in your
mouth a fire, and this people wood, and the fire
shall devour them. Behold, I am bringing upon
you a nation from afar, O house of Israel, says the
Lord...." (Jeremiah 5:12-15)

God says, "I am making my word in your mouth a
fire." Previously we noticed that Jeremiah said, "Your
word has become like fire in my bones." It was burning
inside of him and he couldn't keep quiet. Here God says,
"I am putting My word into your mouth and I am going
to make it like a fire. It will be like a consuming word that
comes out with authority. It is going to consume My people,
because they have rejected Me."

So when Jesus Christ came and preached with
authority and said, "I have come from My Father and I
give you the word of My Father," they said, "He preaches
with authority. That is the way Jeremiah preached."

He also preached with great *power*. That is the same
way that Jeremiah preached. "Fire in my bones. I can't
keep it quiet. It has to come out." Also in Jeremiah 23:29 the
Lord said:

Is not my word like fire, says the Lord, and like a
hammer which breaks the rock in pieces?

"It is with great power that My word comes out through
the mouth of Jeremiah. It is like a hammer that will break

126

the rock in pieces." And so when Jesus Christ preached with that same kind of power, like fire and like a hammer, they said, "This man preaches with power. That is the way Jeremiah preached. Maybe this is Jeremiah come back."

There is a third word in Luke 4 that describes the preaching of Jesus. It is a contrasting word showing the full-orbed approach of the message of Jesus Christ.

> And all spoke well of him, and wondered at the gracious words which proceeded out of his mouth; and they said, "Is not this Joseph's son?" (Luke 4:22)

Jesus Christ preached with authority and power. There were times that His Word came out like fire and like a hammer smashing the rocks to bits. Jesus Christ also preached with *gracious* words. "Grace is poured upon your lips," prophesied the Psalmist (45:2). And the grace of God was poured out through Jesus Christ.

Jeremiah preached the same way. There are many passages in Jeremiah where we see the grace of God coming through.

> Thus says the Lord: "The people who survived the sword found grace in the wilderness; when Israel sought for rest, the Lord appeared to him from afar. I have loved you with an everlasting love; therefore I have continued my faithfulness to you." (Jeremiah 31:2, 3)

> "Behold, the days are coming, says the Lord, when I will make a new covenant with the house of Israel and the house of Judah, not like the covenant which I made with their fathers when I took them by the hand to bring them out of the land of Egypt,

127

my covenant which they broke, though I was their husband, says the Lord. But this is the covenant which I will make with the house of Israel after those days, says the Lord: I will put my law within them, and I will write it upon their hearts; and I will be their God, and they shall be my people." (Jeremiah 31:31-33)

Gracious words! Again in Chapter 33, grace is poured out:

"Thus says the Lord who made the earth, the Lord who formed it to establish it—the Lord is his name: Call to me and I will answer you, and will tell you great and hidden things which you have not known.... Behold, I will bring to it health and healing, and I will heal them and reveal to them abundance of prosperity and security. I will restore the fortunes of Judah and the fortunes of Israel, and rebuild them as they were at first.... And this city shall be to me a name of joy, a praise and a glory before all the nations of the earth who shall hear of all the good that I do for them; they shall fear and tremble because of all the good and all the prosperity I provide for it." (Verses 2, 3, 6, 7, 9)

Words of grace, words of forgiveness, words of comfort from the mouth of Jeremiah.

So when Jesus preached and the people wondered and were astonished at the gracious words that came out of His mouth, they remembered, "Jeremiah preached that way too." In addition to authority and power and judgment, there was the forgiving grace of God in his preaching.

It is a wonderful thing to see the grace of God at work in the lives and the hearts of people.

One of my very dear friends in Colombia is a man named Eliecer Benavides. He has experienced the grace of God in his ministry. It was great to watch him minister, because he had learned the forgiveness of God in a very personal way.

Before he became a Christian, he worked in a gold mine in the mountains of Colombia. Every day he would slip a little gold into his shoe or into his sock and steal it.

Later when he became a Christian, he entered our Bible Institute to prepare for the ministry. One day in class the professor was teaching about Zacchaeus. When Jesus came to his home, Zacchaeus, under conviction of sin, announced that whatever he had stolen from people, he would restore it fourfold. Eliecer came under conviction and went to the teacher after class. He told him what he had done.

He said, "As a Christian I must do something to make this right. What will I do?"

The teacher, Tom Cherry, said to him, "Well, Eliecer, you really have only one choice. You have to write to the owner of that gold mine and tell him what you did. Tell him you want to get it straightened out."

He said, "But they may put me in prison."

"Yes," said Tom, "that might be what you will have to face in order to set this thing right."

So Eliecer sat down and wrote to the owner of the gold mine. He told him what he had done. Then he waited for the police to come and escort him off to jail.

Instead of that, he received a letter from the owner of the gold mine: "In all my life I have never met a man who confessed something like this without being caught. I am so impressed with what you have done and with the fact that you are now studying in a Bible Institute to prepare

for serving God, I'll tell you what I will do. You figure out
how much you stole from me, drop out of school, go to work,
and earn that amount of money. Then give it to the Bible
Institute where you are studying, and I will call it square."

Eliecer dropped out of school, went off into the
country, and began to work. He earned the amount of
money that he thought he had stolen and contributed it to
the school. Then he came back and graduated.

After graduation he went into the backwoods of
Colombia and began to witness. One of the first people he
led to Jesus Christ was a man named Victor Landero. Victor
was used of God in leading his entire family to Jesus Christ
and hundreds of other people in that area too. One of
his brothers that he led to Christ was Gregorio Landero,
who was a major speaker at Urbana 73. Gregorio could speak
at Urbana because the grace of God worked in the heart of
Eliecer years before, and he learned the meaning of
forgiveness.

Several years later Eliecer was working in the Bible
Institute from which he had graduated. One night he was
taken in great temptation and fell into sin. No one knew
about it except the woman with whom he sinned. The next
day he went again to Tom Cherry who had helped him
previously. He broke down, poured out his heart, and
confessed what he had done. Tom embraced him, wept
with him, and prayed with him. But in deep sorrow they
had to dismiss him from the Bible Institute.

Eliecer went back into the hinterlands to work again on
the farm. We kept an eye on him and watched him
develop. We saw him growing. We saw that his confession
and his forgiveness had been complete. His desire to do right
had been genuine. We finally invited him to return and
join us again in the work.

I remember the first time I saw him after he came back. I said to him, "Eliecer, we are so glad that you are back in the ministry with us."

He looked at me with the most incredulous look in his eyes and said, *"Don* David, I can't understand how you could ever invite me back. You know what kind of a man I am. You know what I have done. You know my failures and my weaknesses. How could you bring me back?"

But you see, it was the grace of God that was at work in him. The message of the gracious words of forgiveness through Jesus Christ had reached into his heart and touched his life. He is still in the pastorate today and is carrying on an effective ministry. You may never hear of him publicly, but look for him in heaven. He will be way up in the front lines, wearing a glittering crown of faithfulness. He is a man who knows the grace of God at work.

Jeremiah knew how to preach the grace and forgiveness of God, as well as the power, the authority, and the judgment of God. So when Jesus Christ came and began to preach with authority and with power but also extended His hand of gracious love and forgiveness, the people said, "Look! That is the kind of man Jeremiah was. Maybe this is Jeremiah come back again."

I mentioned previously that prayer meeting in Lausanne. I will never forget the prayer of one man from Sweden. He had been in Russia a number of times and knew the Christians in the underground. He knew many who had suffered. He knew that some had not been able to stand up under severe persecution. He prayed for those Christians in Russia who had given in under the pressures which had become too great for them. Some had been in the slave labor camps and had suffered the

131

kind of things that Solzhenitsyn described. Some cracked under it and gave up their faith.

He prayed for those Christians and said, "Lord, remember those Christians too. They are your children. Lord, help them to know that your grace reaches to them also."

He was conscious that regardless of how deep the sin and how complete the rejection, the grace of God can still reach to them.

You and I in dealing with non-Christians today must bring this same message. We must come with authority. We must come with power. But we must come also with gracious words, so men and women will know that the message we bring is a message of forgiveness and grace, because that is the way Jesus Christ preached.

CHAPTER THIRTEEN

"Great Is Thy Faithfulness"

The Attitude of Jeremiah

We have looked at Jeremiah's personality—a man of sorrows, acquainted with grief, oppressed and afflicted. We have looked at his message—a message of authority, power, grace. What about his attitudes? There are three great virtues mentioned in the New Testament which describe beautifully the attitudes of Jesus Christ, and also of Jeremiah.

Jesus Christ was a man of great *faith*. So was Jeremiah. We noticed previously that incident toward the end of his life in the tenth year of the king Zedekiah. The armies of Nebuchadnezzar were surrounding the city. The walls were crumbling. The city was about to be destroyed and Israel carried off into captivity. In the midst of that, what did Jeremiah do? He bought real estate! Why would anyone do that? Because he had faith that God was going to fulfill His purposes and bring His people back to that land. He knew that this land still belonged to God and to His people. In the midst of impending doom, he expressed his faith and bought that field.

It is always exciting to read church history and see how the Church has stood up in faith during times of deep trial. The history of missions shows the same thing, and sometimes even more dramatically than other parts of church history. It is especially stimulating to read the history of how students have been involved in missions and to find out how God has worked in their lives.

In 1936, the Student Foreign Missions Fellowship, which is now part of Inter-Varsity, was founded. This was at the worst point of the Depression, when mission boards were cutting back their budgets and personnel were being called home. There seemed to be no hope of expanding. The pinch was being felt all over the world.

Then a small group of students from schools in the East and the Midwest stood up and said, "But God's plans will still go forward. We firmly believe that we need to be used of God once again to awaken the Church to its worldwide responsibilities." That small group of about fifty students at a Bible conference organized the Student Foreign Missions Fellowship. Their elders were saying, "Forget it! We aren't going to be sending any more missionaries for years to come. There isn't money to send anyone." But the students believed that God would supply all of their needs according to His riches in glory. And they were right.

Next there is the great virtue of *hope*. Jesus Christ was a man of hope. So was Jeremiah. That lovely hymn, "Great Is Thy Faithfulness," is taken from the words of Jeremiah in Lamentations 3. This expression of hope comes out of the heart of a man in grief. Lamentations was apparently written after Jerusalem fell. Jerusalem was desolate. Jeremiah was lamenting over the fate of the city which had now been destroyed. Perhaps Jeremiah wrote this just before he was taken off to Egypt. Maybe he wrote it after he was carried off in captivity to Egypt. At any rate, in the midst of this mournful dirge over the city he says:

> Remember my affliction and my bitterness, the wormwood and the gall! My soul continually thinks of it and is bowed down within me. But this I call to mind, and therefore I have hope: The steadfast love of the Lord never ceases, his mercies never come to an end; they are new every morning; great is thy faithfulness. "The Lord is my portion," says my soul, "therefore I will hope in him." (Lamentations 3:19-24)

What an expression of hope! After all the destruction, desolation, and rejection which Jeremiah had suffered throughout his life, and after seeing the city destroyed and the people carried off into captivity, he still cries out, "His mercies never come to an end; they are new every morning; great is thy faithfulness ... therefore I will hope in him."

One day at Lausanne in 1974, I had a conversation with an African man. Looking at his name tag, I noticed that his last name was Mohammed. I said, "Does that mean that before you became a Christian, you were a Muslim?"

He said, "Yes, it does."

"Would you tell me how you became a Christian?"

He related how fourteen years previously, when he was a student, he received a New Testament. He said, "I read all the way through it. I got to Revelation 3 and read the letter to the church at Laodicea. God said, 'You are neither

135

hot nor cold; you are lukewarm and I will spew you out of my mouth.'

"I realized that described my religion. I was a practicing Muslim. I said my prayer five times a day towards Mecca. But I was neither hot nor cold. So God said to me, 'I am going to spew you out of my mouth.' It suddenly came home to me that I needed a Savior. Having read the entire New Testament, I knew by that time that the only true Savior was Jesus Christ. So I turned to Jesus Christ."

I said, "What did this mean in your home and family?"

"I was expelled from my home by my parents and rejected by my brothers and sisters. But I knew that I was believing right."

Then he added with a delightful smile on his face, "You know, they aren't Christians yet, but they are going to become Christians. My whole family will be saved sooner or later. One sister is a Christian now, and the rest of them are going to come."

This was a great expression of hope because he knew that God would do His work. So he expressed it with that sense of joy and certainty that God will complete His purposes.

A third great virtue mentioned in the New Testament is *love*. Jesus Christ was the supreme expression of love—the supreme expression of a loving Father to His children. He identified Himself with the human race in the Incarnation, and He came and preached above all else the love of God for His creatures. Men and women listened to Him and they said, "That is the way Jeremiah talked."

Jeremiah also knew how to proclaim the love of God. The preaching of Jeremiah—for all of its judgment and for all of its power and authority—was nevertheless filled with the love of God. "I have loved thee with an everlasting

love: therefore with loving-kindness have I drawn thee"
(Jeremiah 31:3, KJV). That is found right in the heart of the
book of Jeremiah.

Why did Jeremiah weep so often? Jeremiah loved
both God and Israel. Thus there was deep sadness in his
heart as he saw the separation between God who loved His
people, and the people who rebelled against Him.

One of the saddest things in all of human life must be
the broken heart of the small child whose parents are
separated. I thank God that I never had to go through that at
any level of my family life. But many have to face that.
Think what it must mean to the small children who love
both parents when they see those parents going separate
ways. They see hatred and barriers building up between
them. Finally an ultimate break comes. And that little child
is torn because he loves father and he also loves mother.
And father and mother are now at enmity with each other.

That is precisely where Jeremiah was. "I love these people.
They are my people. I identify with them. But they have
rejected their Father, and I love Him because He is my
Father." Jeremiah wept as he saw this divorce take place
between the people of God and their Father. And Jeremiah
poured out his heart in anguish because he was a man of
love.

The people of the New Testament had seen this love in
reading Jeremiah. So when Jesus Christ came and preached
love, the people said, "Yes, yes, that is the way Jeremiah
was! Perhaps this is Jeremiah who has returned."

I wish I could share with you some of the hundreds of
letters received after Urbana 73. For more than a year, hardly
a week passed without our receiving several letters from
students expressing what God did for them at that
convention. It was deeply gratifying to read them and see

137

what God had been doing in the lives of these students. One of the more expressive ones was from a girl in Canada:

> Thank you for your letter concerning my follow-up of Urbana 73. My week there was one of the most moving experiences of my life, because it was there that I became a Christian. I went with a most negative attitude about Christians and made up my mind that nobody was going to change my life or attitude. Well, as soon as I got there, I began to break down the defensive wall I had built around myself. I could feel myself growing and changing every day until finally, on the way home, I committed my life to Christ. As you must know, I've certainly never regretted it, and it's getting better and is growing stronger, warmer, and wilder every day. What I want to say though is, the thing that changed my attitude wasn't what anybody said to me and it wasn't anything that was said at the meetings or assemblies. It was simply the people, the overwhelming genuine love that radiated from every person I met.

And that's what got to her. The overwhelming, genuine love that radiated from every person she met at that convention! Her defenses began to weaken. Finally, on the way home, she could resist no longer and she committed herself to Jesus Christ. It was true love that got through to her.

Jeremiah was a man of great faith. He was a man of great hope. He knew that God would fulfill his purposes, because that is what God said when He first called him. "I am watching over my word to perform it." Jeremiah believed that. He was also a man of great love. It was a brokenhearted kind of love, because of that divorce that took place between God and His people Israel. He poured out his heart in love to his Father and to the people whom he also loved.

Will anyone ever confuse you with Jesus Christ? Will anyone ever look at you and say, "That is the way Jesus Christ was"?